The Denison Family of Toronto

George Taylor Denison 3rd

Photograph courtesy of Ontario Archives

The Denison Family of Toronto
1792-1925

DAVID GAGAN

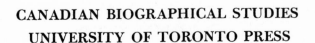

CANADIAN BIOGRAPHICAL STUDIES
UNIVERSITY OF TORONTO PRESS

CANADIAN BIOGRAPHICAL STUDIES

1 John Strachan 1778-1867
J.L.H. Henderson

2 Roland-Michel Barrin de La Galissonière 1693-1756
Lionel Groulx

3 John Sandfield Macdonald 1812-1872
Bruce W. Hodgins

4 Henry Alline 1748-1784
J.M. Bumsted

5 The Denison Family of Toronto 1792-1925
David Gagan

Co-editors Alan Wilson and André Vachon

© University of Toronto Press 1973
Printed in Canada
ISBN 0-8020-3296-6 (Cloth)
ISBN 0-8020-3297-4 (Paper)
Microfiche ISBN 0-8020-0270-6

TO ROSEMARY

Contents

Foreword

The *Canadian Biographical Studies* is allied with the project of the *Dictionary of Canadian Biography/Dictionnaire biographique du Canada.*

These small volumes are designed primarily to interest the general reader, and they will be published in two languages. They seek to fill a gap in our knowledge of men who seemed often to be merely secondary figures, frequently non-political contributors to our regional and national experience in Canada. Our social, educational, and economic history may perhaps be better understood in their light.

In these *Studies*, the emphasis is upon an interpretation rather than a life. The limitation in size challenges the author to consider the best use of anecdote, description of place, reference to general history, and use of quotation. The general reader will be offered the fruits of recent research. Not all of the volumes will aim at full comprehensiveness and completeness: some may be followed later by larger and fuller studies of the subject. Many of the present studies, it is hoped, may suggest new interpretative possibilities not only about the central figure but about his period.

The editors have not followed two of Plutarch's chief standards: the subjects of these *Studies* have not been chosen only for their public virtue, or for their acknowledged distinction. Most of them lived out their lives in Canada, but for some their careers were conducted partly in other theatres. Some have been chosen because, though they were once widely known, they have since been undeservedly neglected. Some have been selected not for their obvious leadership or eminence, but because they were sufficiently prominent to represent some of the qualities that guided their age, men of significance if not of first prominence. Some have been grouped in studies that should throw light on interesting families, professional groups, or lobbies in our past.

Thus, the *Studies* present not biography alone, but social, economic and political history approached through the careers and ideas – acknowledged, but often unrecognized – of Canadians of many ranks and diverse times.

ALAN WILSON

Preface

Anna Jameson, an acerbic critic of Upper Canadian society, ascribed its fundamental characteristics to 'the very first elements out of which our social system was framed ... repugnance and contempt for the new institutions of the United States, and a dislike to the people of that country. ...' She also noted the inhabitants' love and pride for 'high and happy England' which appeared, in her opinion, to supplant their patriotism for Canada. Mrs. Jameson concluded that Upper Canadian society must therefore be weak and rootless. Had she observed more closely she might have discovered that antipathy to the United States of America and pride in Empire represented both the form and the substance of a vigorous British North American patriotism which drew from these two sources the ideological and the institutional bases of a distinct British American identity. This was the tradition of the United Empire Loyalists.

Few historically prominent British North Americans of the nineteenth century espoused that tradition as consistently, or promoted it as assiduously, as the Denison family of Toronto. As a family, and as individuals, they were dedicated to the perpetuation of the historical character of Upper Canada, of British North America, and of the Dominion of Canada as the product of the Loyalist impulse. As citizens of Toronto, soldiers of the Empire, and Canadian patriots, they created for themselves a historical role consistent with their dedication. My purpose here is to study the evolution of the family from their arrival in North America in 1792 to the death of the third George Taylor Denison in 1925, from a perspective that makes their actions within this context properly comprehensible.

Whatever merit this study possesses is due to the assistance and encouragement of several individuals whose contributions I gratefully acknowledge: Alan Wilson as teacher, editor, and friend; Richard Preston of Duke University who supervised my earlier research on the Denisons; Frederick Armstrong, whose enthusiasm for family history proved to be infectious; and the staffs of the Public Archives of Canada, the Provincial Archives of Ontario, and the Metropolitan Toronto Central Library who are the Canadian historian's right hand.

Errors of omission and commission are, however, entirely my responsibility. In this regard, the reader is asked to note that I accept full responsibility for the accuracy of the direct quotations, which conform to the original sources except where it has been necessary to alter pronouns and verb tenses for grammatical consistency. *Sic* and squared parentheses, consequently, have been abandoned for the sake of stylistic economy.

D.P.G.

The Denison Family of Toronto

I

The Denison Family
1792-1925

Esther, Borden, and Lippincott streets, Rusholme Road, Dovercourt Road, Denison and Ossington avenues are thoroughfares
in the heart of metropolitan Toronto. Their names are familiar
enough to native Torontonians, who would associate them with
the area immediately west of Spadina and bounded roughly by
Queen and College. Today, much of the neighbourhood is an
ethnic quarter of new Canadians, and the variety of its languages
seems strangely out of harmony with the area's historical character as the preserve of the staunchly Anglo-Saxon, United Empire Loyalist Denison family.

Immigrant Yorkshiremen who were among Toronto's first citizens, the Denisons cleared the land and established farms and,
because they adhered to the dominant political ideology of Tory
loyalism, became placemen in the hierarchy of power. Succeeding generations of Denisons improved the family's social, economic, and political standing, and, by the middle of the nineteenth century, the Denisons had become local magnates in their

own right, always represented on city council, the senior officers of the Toronto militia, men who consorted with the elite of two continents. The Denisons' wealth was derived from the land, which they farmed and then developed for urban dwellings. As the city grew out to meet their properties in west Toronto, they named the new streets to perpetuate memories important to them: 'Rusholme' and 'Dovercourt' were the names of the estates belonging to George Taylor Denison (2nd) and Richard Lippincott Denison; Esther, Borden and Lippincott streets were named after the grandmother who brought to the family their identity as United Empire Loyalists; and Ossington was a gesture to the belief that the Denisons were a minor branch of the ennobled house of Denison, the Earls of Ossington, in Yorkshire.

For over a century, from 1797 until the death in 1925 of George Denison (3rd), the history of the family and the city were inextricably linked. That in itself seems to be sufficient justification for a biographical study. The historical development of this family is a microcosm of Toronto's growth from a backwoods provincial capital to a major North American metropolis. As a magistrate in the 1830s, George Taylor Denison (1st) was concerned with hogs running loose in the streets; his grandson ended life as Toronto's senior police magistrate grappling with the social problems of a modern urban environment. John Denison, the first Canadian Denison, began life in Toronto managing someone else's farm; his son rented land to more than a hundred tenants, and his grandson developed the same land into urban residential sites. The Denison record, in effect, is the record of an evolving urban community.

In quite a different way, the Denisons are important as representatives of the type of people who sustained the fundamentally conservative character of York and Upper Canada, Toronto and Ontario. Loyalists only by marriage, their political philosophy nevertheless was rooted in the twin streams of Loyalist conservatism. On one hand, the Denisons represented the Tory reaction to the American Revolution, reinforced by the War of 1812. Loyalty to the Crown, the unity of the Empire, and perpetuation of the institutions of constitutional monarchy were barriers to be maintained against revolution, republican democracy, and the threat of anarchy. Similarly, in keeping with the eighteenth-century concepts of politics and society that were imported to British North America after 1791, the Denisons supported the established church; they equated rank with landed wealth, and assumed that it carried with it social and political obligations; and they believed that rational men, men with preconceptions like their own, could construct and govern wisely a well-ordered polity. The Denisons contributed directly to the development of this society as ardent supporters of the militia, the ultimate defenders of the political state. They are not to be confused, however, with the so-called 'Family Compact' except in so far as the Compact represents a readily identifiable distillation of the biases of countless individuals, like the Denisons, who gave the province its historical character.

But the Denisons are also of historical interest in their own right. They were, after all, public men who became protagonists in issues affecting the growth and direction of Canadian nationhood. As soldiers, Loyalists, nationalists, and imperialists they played active roles in the War of 1812, the rebellion of 1837, the militia crises of 1854-1864, the Canada First movement, the 'loyalty crisis' of 1888-1891, and the 'struggle for imperial unity,' 1893-1911. Frederick Denison won personal fame for his part in the attempt to rescue 'Chinese' Gordon from Khartoum in 1884; and George Taylor Denison (3rd) earned an international reputation as a prescient military historian. Not historical characters of the first rank by any means, these individual Denisons nevertheless espoused causes that reflected the concerns of their contemporaries, and from time to time they even attempted to lead public opinion in one direction and thus influence the course of history. In fact, nothing is more certain about the Denisons than their sense of historical occasion; and nothing is more remarkable than the extent to which the family, as an institution with an historical identity of its own, determined the form and extent of the aspirations and attitudes of individual Denisons, and therefore the nature of the historical roles they ultimately played. The Denison motto, *Perseverando,* was not just a platitude emblazoned on the family crest. Every generation of Denisons was challenged not merely to live up to, but to improve upon the family's record of loyalty and patriotism, its standards of personal success and accomplishment.

The transmission of these cultural characteristics from each generation of the family to the next, and the tendency of each generation's experience to reinforce the family's historical experience, created a strong, permanent family identity, and it persisted in spite of the passing of time which inevitably produced changes in the Denisons' social, economic, and demographic characteristics. The ability, and the need, of successive generations of Denisons to identify with an on-going familial tradition in order to understand their own experience provides a fundamental explanation for the recurring themes that unify the history of four generations of the family. It is this underlying unity which provides the focus for the study that follows, and it helps to explain one of the more pressing difficulties, perhaps one might even say shortcomings, of family history.

The Denison family's genealogy now runs to more than twenty printed pages. Yet the experience of the vast majority of these Denisons is beyond recovery for the historian, since the only records that survive are those which every man leaves to posterity, willingly or not, no matter how unique or how common his experience might have been – census data, land transactions, assessments, and his obituary notice. With these resources the historian might reconstruct the skeleton, but not the man. He is therefore inevitably drawn toward the individual whose attitudes and actions, motivations and aspirations have survived the test of time for whatever reasons. Among the Denisons of Toronto, it seems more than mere coincidence that those individuals who are the most visible from the vantage point of the historian also happen to be men who conform most consistently to the family's permanent identity: the line descended from George Taylor Denison of Bellevue. It is true that their social, economic, and political prominence can be explained in terms of fortuitous marriages and some equally happy accidents of history, but in the final analysis it is their perception of, and commitment to a familial tradition, coupled with their desire and ability to foster that tradition, that makes them subjects of special interest to the Canadian historian.

That, at least, is the justification for this study, which has been built around the careers and activities of some half-dozen Denisons, with the rest left in what Peter Lazlett has described as 'the world we have lost.' Nevertheless, these historically prominent Denisons grew with Toronto, with Upper Canada, and with the Dominion, reflecting the changing character of their surroundings in their own development, creating change when the opportunity arose. From the record of their historical experience emerges what is undoubtedly a unique portrait of Canada's past; yet it is one which many of the Denisons' contemporaries would recognize as an equally valid reflection of their own experience, even if the intensity of their involvement in it paled somewhat in comparison to the enthusiasm of this family of warriors, citizens, and patriots.

II

Light cavalry overture

Now my Dear Sir, I am extremely unhappy, as is Mrs. Denison ... for whe
know not what whe shall do for to get into Business for as to attempt to
do anything by ourselves that is impossible as whe have nothing to do it
with. ...[1]

As inspector-general of Upper Canada in 1793, Peter Russell was
accustomed to such complaints from disgruntled settlers. To
carve a new life out of the British North American wilderness
was difficult even for Loyalists conditioned by previous colonial
experience. For the Denison family, recent immigrants from
England, the adjustment was doubly trying, and as John Denison's mentor Russell felt obliged to treat his petitioner with
greater deference than similar pleas might have warranted.

John Denison (1757-1824) was a native of Hedon, Yorkshire.
His wife, Sophia Taylor (1765-1852), was born in Harwich, Suf-
folk. After their marriage, John Denison moved to Alton Hall
where he went into business for himself as a grain farmer who
also served as the community's miller, brewer and coal merchant.

9

He was an experienced militia officer who had served as a lieutenant of light infantry for the West Riding of York. This combination of skills recommended him to Peter Russell, whose half-sister Elizabeth was acquainted with Denison's wife, as 'a very useful acquisition' for the new province of Upper Canada. Before his departure from England as a member of Governor John Graves Simcoe's staff in 1791, Russell induced Denison to abandon his business and emigrate with his wife and sons George, Thomas, and Charles to Upper Canada. The Denisons were promised 'the indulgences allowed to Loyalists.'[2]

Arriving in Kingston in the autumn of 1792, John Denison abruptly abandoned Russell's plan for him to become a farmer and a miller. The area, he thought, held great promise as 'corn country,' and Denison proposed to establish himself as a 'Maltster, Brewer and Distiller' in Edwardsburg. But first he had to acquire the means of realizing his ambition, and he was already in debt, hence his petition to Russell. Could the government be persuaded either to build him a house and brewery or to lend him sufficient money to launch his business? 'If I should be so fortunate as to succeed in this undertaken,' he promised Russell, 'I am not the least afraid but what I should soon be able to supply the Governor and a great part of the country with good Beer. ...'[3]

Though Russell opposed the scheme, he did not ignore Denison's plea for help. Somewhat against his better judgment, the inspector-general advanced Denison a small loan from his own resources. He also secured a land grant for him at York, the site of Simcoe's new provincial capital, perhaps in the hope that the family would move west and make a fresh beginning under improved circumstances. But John Denison was not to be deterred.

Leasing premises from a Joseph Forsythe who also capitalized the venture, Denison established a brewery in Kingston in 1794. No sooner had he put the business on a profitable footing, than Forsythe demanded payment in full of his share of the investment. Unable to disguise his displeasure at Denison's foolishness in allowing himself to be subordinated to a ruthless speculator, Russell flatly rejected Denison's plea for a second loan of £400 with which to purchase the business. Forsythe assumed control of the brewery, leaving John Denison penniless, discouraged, and disillusioned.[4]

To complicate matters, in his anger Peter Russell now threatened to sue Denison to recover his initial loan, still outstanding after three years, unless he sold his land at York to raise the necessary funds. Denison begged for time. Torn between returning to England or attempting to recover his losses, including his friendship with Russell, he finally chose the latter course. 'In the spring,' he informed Russell in November 1796, 'I and my family are going to York to live. ...'[5] Thus began the Denison family's long and intimate identification with Toronto.

When John Denison arrived at York the town, if indeed it deserved the name, consisted of a mere dozen or so rough buildings clustered about lower Yonge Street close to the bay. Still, the task of hewing York's 'parallelogramical' thoroughfares (in Trollope's words) out of the bush was progressing well, and if the town faintly resembled a Roman *castra* accidentally deposited in the wilderness of Upper Canada, it testified equally to the enthusiasm of its founder, Simcoe, who was succeeded as administrator in 1796 by Peter Russell. Happily for John Denison, his removal to York restored his formerly harmonious relationship with Russell, who installed the family in style and comfort in

11

Castle Frank, Simcoe's log and clapboard Greek villa perched high on a cliff overlooking the Don River. Moreover, Russell employed Denison as the manager of Petersfield, his estate which fronted on Lot (now Queen) Street, an occupation demonstrably suited to Denison's talents. Under his direction Petersfield prospered, and Russell rewarded him accordingly with a grant of a thousand acres of land of great speculative value in Grenville County, Eastern District. In time, Denison also bought farm land north of York, near the present town of Weston, and a large park lot to the west of Petersfield near the estates of the Dunns, the Baldwins, and the Ridouts, the civil and military leaders of the community.[6]

Landholding, a lieutenancy in the newly organized York militia, and intimacy with the little group of oligarchs who comprised York's colonial aristocracy, all contributed to John Denison's transition from unhappy immigrant to gentleman farmer. But if he enjoyed the 'indulgences' permitted to Loyalists, the patronage of the province's leading citizen, and the material attributes of a country squire, he and his family did not possess the essential symbol of preferment which, in the long term, distinguished the truly elite from the common immigrant. In Upper Canada, the elect were those who bore, either in their own right or by marriage or descent, the 'Marke of Honour,' the right conferred on the United Empire Loyalists and their descendants to style themselves 'U.E.' When John Denison's eldest son, George Taylor Denison (1783-1853), married Esther Borden Lippincott, U.E., in 1806, the Denison family's ascendancy was virtually complete.

Esther Lippincott (1791-1823) brought more to the Denisons than the privilege of styling themselves as United Empire Loyalists. She and her father Richard Lippincott, who lived with his son-in-law until his death in 1826, carried within them a particularly virulent strain of loyalism which manifested itself as a pathological hatred of Yankee 'rebels.' The hatred was born of Lippincott's experience during the American revolutionary war in which he fought as a captain in the New Jersey Volunteers. These irregulars were one of many 'associated bands' of Tory 'raiders' or guerrillas whose disdain for the 'recognized laws of war' made them feared and hated by the rebels.[7] The upshot was a history of atrocities committed by both sides. Richard Lippincott, for example, learned in the spring of 1782 that his brother-in-law Philip White had been taken from his Shrewsbury, New Jersey, home by force, made to run a gauntlet of rebels, and then shot and mutilated. White's body reportedly was found with one arm cut off, one eye pulled out, and both legs broken. Lippincott immediately requested, and received, permission from the Board of Associated Loyalists in New York to exchange three rebel prisoners for a number of Loyalists held captive in New Jersey, men who might suffer a fate similar to White's. But one of the rebels never reached the appointed rendezvous. The New Jersey Exchange Commissioners shortly informed the board that Captain Joshua Huddy had been found hanged at Sandy Hook on the Jersey shore. Pinned to his breast was a note: 'Up Goes Huddy for Philip White.'

At his subsequent court-martial, which General George Washington demanded of the British commander-in-chief Sir Henry Clinton, Lippincott successfully pleaded that, as a civilian serving without pay, he was not subject to military law. Accordingly, Clinton turned him over to Chief Justice William Smith for trial in the civilian courts. But Smith, a staunch Loyalist himself, de-

13

creed that he could not deal with a crime alleged to have taken place where the Crown's authority was non-existent. He dismissed the case. Nevertheless, Clinton was forced to hold Lippincott in custody for the duration of the war to prevent Washington from exacting his revenge on an officer in Lord Cornwallis' captive army.[8]

After the revolution, Lippincott found his way to Penfield, New Brunswick, and then to England where he lobbied for a half pay commission in the British army in recognition of his loyalty and service. Successful, he returned briefly to New Brunswick, and then in 1793 moved his family to the new Loyalist province of Upper Canada where he had acquired, again for services rendered, a grant of 3,000 acres of land in Vaughan Township near the present village of Richmond Hill. Richard Lippincott's land became the basis of George Denison's fortune, and his 'Marke of Honour' established the Denison family's credentials as Loyalists in principal as well as in fact. But above all, Lippincott's revolutionary experiences, his superlative example of loyalty and devotion to king and country, and his legacy of bitter enmity toward the United States of America, helped subsequent generations of Denisons to define and consolidate their place in the political and social scheme of things in British North America. They raised 'loyalism' to the level of divine injunction, and dedicated themselves to the maintenance of a thoroughly British society in northern North America, a society sentimentally and politically linked to the Empire for which the Loyalists had willingly endured privation and hardship. The Denisons accepted as well that British North America's separate and distinct existence on the continent, and the unity of the Empire, could be threatened in the future from only one quarter, as it had been in 1776. Consequently, they early translated their 'loyalism' into a thoroughly pragmatic concept of duty and responsibility, military service in defence of Upper Canada against those who would thwart what George Taylor Denison (3rd) later defined as 'the dream of the United Empire Loyalists.'

The war of 1812 tested the loyalty of all Upper Canadians under conditions almost as extreme as those that prevailed in 1776, and the Denisons were not found wanting. On the eve of war, Major-General Sir Isaac Brock enlisted the support of the 'Loyal, Brave and Respected Young Men' of the province to create 'flank companies' of more certain loyalty than the regular militia units whose ranks were dominated by recent American immigrants. The young Tories who served in the flank companies reaped no reward beyond the satisfaction of personal dedication to a heroic figure, Brock, and to the defence of Upper Canada in the hour of peril. Both George Taylor Denison and his brother Charles (1789-1828) served with the York flank companies, often performing hazardous escort and despatch duty. George saw action at Detroit and during the brief but relatively bloodless defence of York, in 1813, where he was captured and held prisoner for six months. Consequently, the repetition of familial historical experience, of once again defending king and country against *the* aggressor, and in a capacity by definition more patriotic than the exertions of common men, would be alluded to thereafter as an object lesson in history and in the duty of men toward the state.[9]

After the war, the ultrapatriotic spirit of Upper Canada's second generation Loyalists dominated the political and social climate of the province. Thus, when the decision was taken in 1822 to attach troops of volunteer cavalry to the militia infantry regiments, the loyal young men of the better class who had performed an especially patriotic function during the late war again came forward to organize the troops. At York, Captain George Taylor Denison created the York Dragoons attached to the West York Regiment of Militia. Dressed in the blue and buff uniforms of H.M. 13th Light Dragoons and led by youthful squires who possessed the means to acquire the trappings of chivalry, the York Dragoons were an object of local pride as they performed Sunday drill on Garrison Common or paraded to church with their commander.[10]

But the York Dragoons existed for political as well as ceremonial purposes. In keeping with the Denison family's political leanings and their congenital feud with the United States and its revolutionary ideology, the troop was in the vanguard of the loyal forces who rallied to the defence of York against William Lyon Mackenzie's rag-tag republicans in December 1837. George Denison, his eldest son Richard Lippincott (1814-1878), and brother Tom (1786-1846) mustered the Dragoons and a force of volunteer infantry to defend Fort York. Subsequently, the York Dragoons were pressed into active service with the British army. Employed in escort and despatch duty throughout the winter of 1837-1838, they were given the honorary designation 'Queen's Light Dragoons' in recognition of their performance. Meanwhile, George Taylor Denison (2nd) (1816-1873) and a small body of Dragoons who had helped to break the back of the rebellion in the battle of Gallows Hill on 7 December were attached to Sir Allan MacNab's force which pursued the fleeing insurgents into western Ontario and then laid siege to the rebel stronghold on Navy Island in the Niagara River.

The end of the rebellion and the return of political stability to the province nearly brought about the demise of the York Dragoons. When the active force was disbanded in 1839, the troop was forced to return to stores all its equipment, which belonged to the imperial government. A substantial body of troopers could not be sustained without it. At the same time, George Taylor Denison (Sr.) was promoted to lieutenant-colonel commanding the First West York Battalion, thereby ending his affiliation with the Dragoons. Undaunted, his sons, Captain Richard Lippincott Denison, Lieutenant George Taylor Denison (2nd), and Cornet Robert Brittain Denison (1821-1900), decided to purchase the necessary equipment for the Dragoons out of their own pockets. Shakos, sabres, sabre belts, ammunition pouches, and jackets were all acquired and loaned to the troopers who posted bond against loss or damage. As 'owners' of the troop, the Denisons naturally exercised their right to fill the highest ranks, and of the twenty-one officers holding commissions in the troop before 1876, eleven were Denisons. More remarkably, the troop was consistently under the command of a Denison until 1902. Appropriately, the Queen's Light Dragoons soon enjoyed popular identification as 'Denison's Horse.'[11]

Perhaps William Lyon Mackenzie had the Denisons, among others, in mind when he railed in his 'Independence' manifesto against 'Captains, Colonels, Volunteers, Artillerymen and Privates' as the 'hirelings' of the Family Compact.[12] The Denisons had assumed the posture of a military elite, interpreting their role as Upper Canada's first line of defence against external aggression and internal treachery. In so doing, they contributed, as did others like them, to the maintenance of the province's per-

vasive Tory substructure which gave the ruling oligarchy its necessary strength and support.[13] Still, if the Denisons were in
many ways typical of the lower ranks of entrenched Toryism in
Upper Canada, they were too ambitious, too independent to remain mere placemen in a society open at the top to the talented
and the industrious. Their ability, desire, and right to maintain
and lead what was virtually a troop of household cavalry testified equally to the diligent industry of the second and third generations of Denisons.

George Taylor Denison of Bellevue (so designated to distin-
guish him from his son and grandson of the same name) was one
of the wealthiest landowners in Upper Canada. At his death in
1853 his estate was probated in excess of £200,000, a substantial fortune even by present standards. The basis of his wealth
was land inherited from Richard Lippincott and from his father
whose will, inexplicably, assigned the bulk of his estate to
George Denison, leaving George's brothers Charles and Thomas
without so much as clear title to the farm land they worked.
Sophia Denison was convinced that it had all been a terrible mistake, the result of her husband's refusal to have his will drawn
up by a lawyer.[14] Whatever the reason, there was an irreparable
breach in the family, and an unexpected windfall for George
Denison of Bellevue. Building on this base, he swiftly acquired
additional land in surrounding townships, land soon occupied
by more than a hundred tenant farmers. His own home, 'Bellevue,' a Georgian manor whose gleaming white exterior and shut-
tered windows belied New England's influence on the tastes of
affluent Upper Canadians, stood barely visible at the point where
Denison Avenue, running north from Queen Street, merged with
the receding forest. From his estate, George Denison commanded

the York Dragoons, promoted the Anglican Church with uncommon devotion, energetically participated in local politics,
and bred the finest horses in the province. A 'bluff, hale, strongly
built' man who outlived three of his four wives and six of his
thirteen children, George Denison, to those like Samuel Thompson who knew him well, seemed to be the very image of an English squire from the age of Addison and Steele.[15]

Prior to the incorporation of the city of Toronto in 1834,
George Denison of Bellevue had been one of four magistrates
of the Court of Quarter Sessions of the Peace appointed to
superintend the civil administration of the Home District. That
office, bestowed by the lieutenant-governor, normally testified
to the incumbent's social standing and to the propriety of his
political convictions. The magistrates' responsibilities frequently
tended to revolve around the more commonplace aspects of pioneer life – establishing the weekly price of bread, the problem
posed by the numerous swine allowed to run at large, petty
crimes – but in dealing even with these matters they were mold-
ing the shape of the city to be. Having acquired, in this capacity,
a reputation as 'a fair magistrate,' George Taylor Denison was
returned as alderman for St. Patrick's Ward in the first civic election after the incorporation. He was a tower of Tory strength in
a council strictly divided on partisan lines and presided over by
William Lyon Mackenzie, Toronto's erratic first mayor. Denison's attitude toward Mackenzie was as visceral as that of any
of his class. Colonel William O'Brien had noted in his diary in
1830 that when Mackenzie tried to force his way into a meeting
of the Agricultural Society, it was George Denison who volunteered to restrain the editor of the *Colonial Advocate* 'by giving
him a slap in the chops.'[16]

A 'sound and consistent churchman' who established the Denison family's reputation as inveterate church builders and active Anglican laymen, George Denison regarded the Church of England as the state church of Upper Canada, a bulwark of the social and political structure of the province. So deep was his conviction that, in 1853, on the eve of the secularization of the clergy reserves, which struck the Denisons as 'an unchristian movement,' George Denison entailed a portion of his estates to provide an endowment for the church of St. John's-on-the-Humber near Weston. It thus became an ecclesiastical living in the perpetual gift of the Denison family, as did St. Stephen's-in-the-Fields on College Street, similarly endowed by his son Robert Brittain Denison, the second master of Bellevue.[17]

In this, as in every respect, George Taylor Denison of Bellevue established a pattern for his sons, and they conformed to their father's squirarchical mold. 'Rusholme,' the estate of George Taylor Denison (2nd), and 'Dover Court,' Richard Lippincott Denison's farm, lay to the west of Bellevue. Later to be joined by 'Heydon Villa' of George Taylor Denison (3rd), they occupied most of the area now encompassed by Queen Street, College Street, Dufferin Street, and Ossington Avenue; but even in mid-century they were situated in baronial splendour amid fields and forests of cedar and pine, on land drained by Garrison Creek which traversed the properties on its way to Lake Ontario. These 'populous colonies' of Denisons, as the Reverend Dr. Scadding described them, virtually constituted a separate and distinct community on the western edge of Toronto, and in fact the families tended toward clannishness. That is not to say, however, that the Denisons' outlook was 'circumscribed,' as one visitor characterized the Torontonians he met in 1847, 'by the visible horizon.'[18] Rather, George Denison's sons were characteristic of the rising generation of well-educated young men whose entrepreneurial zeal and skill, and urbanity, were to mark Toronto's emergence as the commercial and intellectual hub of Laurentian Canada.

Richard Lippincott Denison and Robert Brittain Denison were both fine examples of the type. Richard was not only a successful farmer with vast acreages, but a businessman with investments, and offices, in mortgage, mining, and insurance companies. He was also a patron of the arts and sciences, particularly agricultural science, and for that reason was appointed as the province of Canada's commissioner to the Paris Exposition in 1855. With perhaps a touch of irony intended, he was also Toronto's official representative to the Philadelphia exposition held in 1876 in conjunction with the centennial of American independence.[19] Robert, who inherited Bellevue, seems to have divided his energies equally between the provincial militia and church-building. He personally underwrote the costs of St. Stephen's, and he rose from the rank of cornet in his father's troop to become deputy adjutant-general of the Canadian militia. Both brothers, like their father, also served their turn as aldermen for St. Patrick's.[20]

Perhaps none of the sons of George Taylor Denison of Bellevue embraced the new and the older orders with a facility equal to that of George Taylor Denison (2nd) of Rusholme. A farmer by inclination, he retained his grandfather's attachment to the soil, lavishing care and time on the fields and orchards of Rusholme which became a model of productive, scientific farming. On the other hand, as a lawyer and entrepreneur he amassed a fortune nearly the equal of his father's. Denison consorted socially with princes, governors-general, and ministers of the Crown, yet he thought nothing of engaging publicly in a fist-fight with an Upper Canada College master who had disciplined his little brother, or of tramping the woods in search of squirrels and pigeons to augment the family larder. In all, George Denison of Rusholme reflects the image of a colonial society in transition.

One of the first graduates of Upper Canada College, George Denison (2nd) entered the legal profession in 1834 under articles to George Cartwright Strachan, son of the Archdeacon of York. Denison's father became dissatisfied with the firm, however, ostensibly because its small clientele restricted his son's opportunity for advancement, and in 1837 the younger Denison transferred to the firm of Edward Hitchings. Admitted to the bar of Upper Canada in 1839 as a barrister, Denison began his own practice in 1840 and soon numbered the leading citizens of Toronto, including Strachan, now the Bishop, among his clients. Sixteen years later, at forty, he voluntarily closed his offices and retired from the legal profession in order to devote all his energies to other enterprises from which he had derived, in the meantime, immense wealth.[21]

Land was also the foundation of this George Denison's fortune. Like his father, he had acquired farms and tenants whose rents, in a period when specie was scarce, frequently were commuted to goods and labour services. One tenant supplied firewood or painted Rusholme, another assisted with the sowing and harvesting of the tobacco crop, and still another mended fences or perhaps spent a few days hauling gravel to surface Bay Street, York, or Spadina, work for which George Denison was the successful contractor. Denison was able, consequently, to run an extensive farming operation with low overhead costs, thereby realizing a healthy return on the tobacco, field crops, orchard produce, cattle and swine that he raised for both the local and the export markets. More significantly, by mid-century land values in Toronto had appreciated drastically as the result of urban growth. By 1853, undeveloped Denison park lots, for example land north of Dundas Street originally acquired at little or no cost by John Denison, were worth from £100 to £300 per acre. George Denison astutely developed his own land and the 1500 acres he and his brothers had inherited from their father and held jointly under a loosely organized family corporation, into fashionable residential properties. He also built row housing on land leased perpetually, under very favourable terms, from the city of Toronto. George Denison seems, in fact, to have been the prime mover behind West Toronto's urban development, and from it acquired the means of perpetuating, indeed enhancing, the traditional family image of landed gentility.[22]

George Denison's style in the 1850s and 1860s reflected his own financial success and the increasing sophistication of Torontonians. The carriage he bought for his wife Anne (Mary Anne Dewson 1817-1900) was 'generally admitted by everyone who sees it to be the finest and most genteel twin set in Toronto.'[23] It was no match, however, for his own coach emblazoned with the family crest and attended, when the occasion demanded it, by liveried coachmen. A concert by Jenny Lind, a performance of *Il Trovatore*, the racing meets of the Toronto Turf Club, especially the 'Queen's Plate' which Denison, as an officer of the club, was instrumental in establishing in 1860 as the classic of Canadian thoroughbred races, were typical events of the Denisons' social life. So too were the countless winter

soirées, gala balls in the Continental manner held for the amuse-
ment of Toronto's aristocracy of wealth and place, the Drapers,
the Mowats, the Robinsons, the Gzowskis, the Tyrwhitts and
half a hundred other families belonging to the privileged set.
At one such ball in September 1860 Denison's daughter Lilla
waltzed with the visiting Prince of Wales. A year later she, and
her sisters, were presented at court during the family's first trip
to England and the Continent. And yet, in spite of all the advantages that his wealth and social position conferred on his family,
George Denison appears to have remained an essentially uncom-
plicated man who delighted in simple pastimes, hunting in the
woods of West Gwillimbury township where his wife's family
lived, never failing to be on hand for local 'firsts' such as the
arrival of the first steam locomotive, or challenging a neighbour
to match a prized pacer and cutter against his long-legged son
George over a half-mile course on the ice of Lake Ontario. The
horse lost.[24]

George Denison's political activities were confined to local af-
fairs where he earned a reputation as an outspoken opponent of
the new breed of politicians cast up by the railroad era in Canada
West. After a decade of service as alderman for St. Patrick's, in
1853 he led seven other members in resigning over Mayor J.G.
Bowes' complicity in Prime Minister Francis Hincks' '£10,000
Job,' a scandal involving Northern Railroad bonds. Denison
seems to have had no further political aspirations, although as
early as 1851 he became a supporter of the idea of a federal
union of the Canadas to replace the legislative union of 1841.
But unlike many Upper Canadians who were beginning to chafe
under the restraints of the union because it imposed a balance
of power between French and English Canada, and who there-

fore wished to be free to pursue an independent political destiny, George Denison's interest in federal union stemmed from more immediate circumstances. The recent annexation crisis of 1849, the reappearance of Papineau and Mackenzie in the provincial political arena, and the emergence of the 'republican' Clear Grit faction all convinced him that the forces of continentalism were lining up for a massive assault on the British connection in order to pave the way for Canada's annexation to the United States. A federal union, he thought, might open the way for a happier working relationship between those forces in Canada East and Canada West who, by co-operating politically, could preserve the country's political integrity. They would make a federal party composed of all the 'true subjects of the Crown' including those 'who formerly cried out for Responsible Government ... the Orangemen & the church unions and the Loyal French in Lafontaine's party. ...'[25] Presumably, the Tory merchants of Montreal were quite beyond the pale of redemption.

George Denison's reasonably prescient forecast of the drift of political realignments in the united province after 1850 suggests that the Denisons, like many of their peers, were gradually shedding their arch-Toryism under the impact of altered political and economic circumstances. The trend emerges clearly in the posture that George Denison and his sons adopted on military questions during the following decade and a half of crises prompted by the Crimean War, the American Civil War, and the consequent Anglo-American hostility which eventually propelled the British North American provinces into confederation in 1867.

The advent of colonial self-government in 1849 was in part a by-product of Britain's desire to free herself, for economic and political reasons, from her traditional commitment to defend her far-flung colonial empire. Afterward, the Canadian and imperial governments were driven rapidly into diametrically opposed constitutional postures on the question of responsibility for defence. For the next twenty years, in spite of the province's growing insecurity on the continent, a succession of parsimonious Canadian governments vacillated between support for a relatively inexperienced but nevertheless efficient volunteer force, and maintaining a costly, permanent militia establishment. With the exception of a brief honeymoon during the Crimean War crisis, which led to the Militia Act of 1855 embodying the best elements of the volunteer and regular militia traditions, the relationship between the politicians and the proponents of a viable native defence establishment were studiously cool.[26] Within this context, the Denisons ceased to be merely a military appendage of the political establishment and became an independent, highly critical force for the creation of a military establishment consistent with Canada's new constitutional freedom and responsibility and with the instability of her geographical situation. Moreover, the Denisons tried to set both the pace and the quality of change by personal example.

The Militia Act of 1846 had reinstituted the active militia based on voluntary enlistments from the sedentary militia; but the government's failure to provide funds with which to pay, equip, or drill volunteer units of cavalry threatened to rob the united province of what the Denisons, at least, considered to be its most effective defence. George Taylor Denison of Rusholme, who became commanding officer of Denison's Horse in 1848, promptly regazetted his troop as a volunteer unit, the 1st Toronto Independent Troop of Cavalry, and personally assumed the entire expense of maintaining it, notwithstanding popular and official opposition. 'He received no encouragement from the Government of the day,' his son later recalled, 'even the people of the town discouraged volunteering, thinking it useless ... and when the men appeared in uniform they were laughed at for being soldier mad.'[27] Evidently, the public contempt accorded to the motley array of ill-kempt and frequently inebriated sedentary militia who were mobilized for one day's training each year was transferred, without distinction, to the comparatively well-disciplined volunteers.

In spite of the apathy and criticism that greeted his efforts, George Denison persisted, devoting his considerable energies, talent, leisure time, and wealth not only to the volunteer cavalry but to the other arms of the militia as well. In 1855 he created the Toronto Field Battery, the first artillery unit to be attached to the Toronto militia, and in 1860 was responsible for organizing the now famous 2nd Battalion of Infantry ('Queen's Own' Rifles). In fact, in his own estimation (the sin of pride was not one that the Denisons recognized), George Denison was 'literally the father and founder of the Volunteer Force at Toronto & the surrounding Townships.'[28] But parenthood without help from the government proved to be too great a burden even for George Denison. Not surprisingly, the indecision which characterized the defence policies of both the Macdonald–Cartier and the Sandfield Macdonald-Sicotte governments in the province of Canada during the critical years of the American Civil War prompted an outraged response from the Denisons who resorted to a new weapon to achieve their objectives, public opinion.

Young George Taylor Denison 3rd (1839-1925), a budding military historian, issued three pamphlets in rapid succession. The first two, *Canada: Is She Prepared for War?* and *The Na-*

tional Defences, appeared in the wake of the *'Trent* Crisis' of 1861, setting off a storm of newspaper controversy over the fact and fiction of the likelihood of war. The pamphlets deliberately appealed to the incipient nationalism of British North Americans by comparing the prospect of self-determination, protected by a spirit of militarism and a greatly expanded defensive capacity, with the inevitable consequences of a successful invasion by a power representing 'revolutionary doctrines run wild.' The third pamphlet, *A Review of the Militia Policy of the Present Administration,* was written in response to the defeat of John A. Macdonald's Militia Bill of 1862, and to the succeeding administration's failure to go beyond providing for additional reserves of unpaid, untrained militia in the face of growing American hostility toward British North America. Prime Minister John Sandfield Macdonald, Denison contended, had no more right to control the militia than he had 'to preside over a college of Chaldean astrologists' because his 'ignorance of military matters was so great that he was unable to perceive how ignorant he really was.'[29]

The principal object of these polemics was to promote the creation of a 'national' military force as an instrument of British North America's sovereignty, chiefly as a convincing show of strength and determination for the benefit of the Americans; but given the conspicuous lack of leadership by the provincial government, indeed its unconcern about the militia, George Denison's outpourings may also be taken as an institutionally biased criticism of the government on behalf of men who had a vested interest in the future of the province's military establishment. Nevertheless, the Denisons, and others like them, were genuinely concerned for the safety of their society, and for the future security of the new nation whose birth was imminent and whose character they tried to anticipate by promoting the growth of the military as a continuing force for the preservation of 'the dream of the United Empire Loyalists' in a new political framework.

Unfortunately for George Denison (2nd) and his sons, their habit of speaking their minds about the government, publicly and privately, won them few friends among politicians who, whether the Denisons liked it or not, could grant or withhold favours and privileges to which the Denisons laid claim as their just reward for their efforts. Thus, when the government proposed in 1866 to confer on the Fourth Troop of Royal Guides (Montreal) the honorary designation 'Governor-General's Body Guard,' the wrath of the Denisons descended on the heads of Governor-General Lord Monck and Colonel Patrick MacDougall, the adjutant-general. Only after Major George Taylor Denison (3rd) and all his men threatened to resign from the militia was the honour conferred instead on the First York Light Dragoons (as the troop had been renamed in 1855). Within a fortnight the troop was regazetted under its new designation and with an appropriate motto, *Nulli Secundus* ('Second to None').[30] This heavy dragoonery was not always successful, however, in winning the day for the Denisons. Although he was commandant of the 5th and 10th Military Districts and the senior militia officer in Ontario at Confederation, Colonel George Denison (2nd) coveted the post of deputy adjutant-general for the Dominion of Canada. Not even a petition to Queen Victoria, praying for the post as a reward not only for his own 35 years of service but also in recognition of the loyalty of his grandfathers, father, and uncles, could wring that office out of the government from whom he had suffered, he once said, 'the grossest indignities.'[31]

The Militia Act of 1868, an act designed to promote military organization consistent with the Dominion of Canada's national sovereignty, went far toward promoting the type of military establishment demanded by the Denisons and other volunteer officers. The volunteers, in fact, became Canada's first line of defence. At the same time, they were unhappy with the system because it exempted most citizens from military service, yet offered neither financial relief nor professional careers to the volunteers in return for their mounting obligations and the professional qualifications required of them. Although the Denisons' zeal for soldiering in no way slackened as a result, it is apparent that the limited horizons for advancement held out by the Canadian militia forced the fourth generation of Denisons, the sons of George Denison of Rusholme, either to compromise their plans to pursue the military careers for which they had been trained or to realize their ambitions elsewhere.

Of George and Anne Denison's nine children, seven were sons: George Taylor, Fred, Clarence, John, Henry, Septimus Junius Augustus, and Egerton. The boys enjoyed all the advantages that their father's wealth and station could provide: excellent schooling, professional training, a rigorous education in the military arts under the tutelage of their father and their maternal grandfather, Major Jeremiah Dewson who was a veteran of Waterloo, and commissions in the Body Guard. They were raised, in short, to be Denisons. Still, their ability to duplicate the patterns of success established by their father and grandfather was limited not only for the reasons cited above but also because they were the products of an environment that had changed drastically since the days of their father's youth. They may have been the sons of a gentleman farmer, but they were themselves urbanites whose aspirations were shaped as much by the conditions of city life and the opportunities provided by the professions as by familial tradition. Thus, George and Fred studied law, Clarence and Henry embarked on careers in banking, and John, Septimus, and Egerton became professional soldiers.

The younger generation of Denisons brought to their chosen careers all the enthusiasm and ambition that had become a hallmark of the Denison family. John Denison (1853-1939) is especially noteworthy since he became the first Canadian to fly an admiral's pennant over a British fleet. John had to be pushed into the Royal Navy, and the British government had to be begged to take him in, as a midshipman in 1867. After an uphill struggle to adapt to the seafaring tradition he was rewarded for his diligence in 1893 with the command of the royal yacht *Victoria and Albert*. When he retired in 1909, 'Gentleman John' had reached the rank of rear admiral.[32] Meanwhile, in the other arm of the service his brother Septimus was well on his way to a generalship.

Among the first cadets to pass out of Canada's Royal Military College, Septimus Denison (1859-1937) joined the South Staffordshire Regiment of the British army, retiring voluntarily in 1883 with the rank of major. Discontented with civilian life after a brief and unfruitful business career in Toronto, he was commissioned as an officer in the Royal Canadian Regiment in 1888. From 1893 until 1898 he served as aide-de-camp to the Governor-General of Canada, Lord Aberdeen, and then volunteered for service in South Africa in 1899. There Denison was seconded into the British army as aide-de-camp to Field Marshal Lord Roberts of Kandahar who twice mentioned him in despatches, praise enough to win Denison a C.M.G. from the British government, but insufficient to merit the promotion from lieutenant-colonel to general officer he thought he deserved. 'Lord R. accepted Septimus Denison at his own valuation,' explained General Hutton, the commanding officer of the Canadian militia, in denying the promotion. 'All the Denisons are the same – they are not to be trusted.'[33] Hutton may not have known that the ill feeling was entirely mutual. In any event, Septimus persisted and finally attained the rank of major-general and chief of staff, Western Ontario Command, Canadian Permanent Forces; he was stationed in London, where his favourite sport, 'riding to hounds,' is still followed with unusual enthusiasm.[34]

The brothers who remained in Toronto, especially George and Fred, were no less ambitious, although making his way in the world proved to be a difficult struggle for George. As elder sons who were close to their father and who, as children, had known and revered their grandfather, George Denison of Bellevue, they tended toward an existence that combined habits dictated by their own interests with a life style and obligations that devolved upon them through the persistence of familial traditions. Involvement in local politics, an obligation to devote time and money to command and maintain the Body Guard, duties to perform for the extended 'family' of Denisons in West Toronto were functions that necessarily fell to them while they laboured at the same time not only to emulate, but even to surpass their father's achievements and to live up to his expectations.

As were his brothers, Frederick Denison (1846-1896) was formally educated at Upper Canada College. After graduation he read law, then formed a legal partnership with his older brother

George whose other pursuits as an officer, author, immigration commissioner, sometime politician, and, eventually, police magistrate of Toronto, severely restricted his ability to participate fully in the practice. Consequently, the burden of work and, in time, the practice itself fell to Fred Denison who built a thriving business. After his father's death in 1873 he acquired Rusholme as well and settled into a comfortable existence which afforded him time for his military and political interests. Because all the available commissions in the Body Guard had been taken up by his brothers and cousins, Fred Denison first volunteered in 1865 as a lieutenant in the 2nd Administrative Battalion. Six months later he was able to transfer to his brother George's troop, just in time to participate in their frantic dash to the frontier when the Fenians invaded in 1866. While stationed on the Niagara peninsula, Denison met Colonel Garnet Wolseley, then quartermaster-general for the British garrison in Canada. In 1870, when Wolseley was given the command of the expeditionary force sent to restore order in Manitoba after the Red River uprising, he asked Fred Denison to be his orderly officer. Long afterward, Wolseley remembered the force's tortuous journey by canoe from Thunder Bay to Lake of the Woods as a superhuman effort unparalleled in British military experience. For his part in the expedition, Fred Denison was asked to remain in the new province of Manitoba for nearly a year as aide-de-camp to Lieutenant-Governor Adams Archibald.

In 1872, Denison assumed the command of the Governor-General's Body Guard; but he resigned in 1876 to accommodate his brother George who was vying for a prize offered by the Russians for the best history of cavalry, and who therefore required a commission sufficiently impressive to win favour with the generals of St. Petersburg. Fred turned to local politics as a ready outlet for his energies. As alderman for St. Stephen's Ward from 1878 until 1884 he compiled such a creditable record that, according to rumour, his election as mayor of Toronto in 1885 was virtually assured. But late in August 1884, in the course of a quiet weekend vacation at his summer home across the lake in Chippawa, Denison received a telegram from the office of the Governor-General, Lord Lansdowne. Would he serve as commanding officer of a contingent of Canadian *voyageurs* to be raised for service with a British army that would attempt to rescue General C.G. 'Chinese' Gordon from the embattled Sudanese fortress Khartoum? The proposal came directly from Sir Garnet Wolseley, his old commander, now Baron Wolseley of Cairo and Wolseley, adjutant-general. Denison unhesitatingly agreed, and within two months found himself in Egypt in the company of many veterans of the Red River Expedition who, with Wolseley, again would attempt the impossible.[35]

In response to the events of 1883-1884 which led to General Gordon's entrapment in Khartoum by the fanatical Mahdists,[36] General Wolseley had prepared a memorandum in April 1884 on the route to be followed by a relief expedition. Wolseley had discounted several possible land routes and instead proposed to transport an army up the Nile in small boats 'as we sent the little expeditionary force from Lake Superior to Fort Garry on the Red River in 1870.'[37] Debate raged through the spring and summer of 1884, but, in the end, Wolseley and his 'ring' of advisers prevailed against the recommendations of the men on the spot who preferred a land route. 'Water is water and rock is rock, whether they be in America or Africa,' Colonel W.F. Butler, another Red River veteran, confidently assured Wolseley, 'and the conditions which they can assume towards each other are much the same all the world over.'[38] The only difficulty would be to collect sufficient boats of the right variety, and experienced men to man them, and to have the expedition at Wady Halfa, at the foot of the Second Cataract, early in October in order to be within striking distance of Khartoum by Christmas. It was already mid-August when the British government finally was convinced that only a military expedition could save Gordon. Immediately, the call went out to Britain's boatbuilders for eight hundred modified whale gigs, to West Africa for native *kroomen* to man them, and to Canada for Denison and the *voyageurs* around whose skill in the white water of the Dominion's wilderness rivers Wolseley's strategy revolved.

There is no explanation for Wolseley's preference for Fred Denison as commander of the *voyageurs* apart from his recollection of the camaraderie they shared during the Red River Expedition. In fact, George Denison assumed that Wolseley's message had been intended for him. Certainly Fred Denison was not the same young man, anxious for adventure, that Wolseley had known in 1870. Approaching forty, with family, business, and civic responsibilities, a man who had not seen active duty since 1870 and whose military activities for over a decade had consisted merely of summer training camps, Fred Denison made an apparently illogical comrade-in-arms for men who had been fighting one colonial war after another for fifteen years. Nor was Denison under any official obligation, as a Canadian militia officer, to serve with the British relief expedition. Yet without question this middle-aged lawyer traded the comforts of a pleasant summer's vacation for the heat and dust of the Sudanese 'winter.' There, in spite of the aura that surrounded the heroic at-

tempt to rescue Gordon, his job was to be anything but romantic. Suffering from chronic dysentery that nearly killed him,
Denison engaged in the same physically demanding labour as the
men he led, counting himself fortunate merely to have witnessed
a battle on one occasion. Yet he was convinced that a question
of national pride was involved not only in being asked, but in
being prepared to serve the cause of Empire. A Denison had no
other choice but to go.

When Fred Denison arrived in Ottawa to assist in organizing
the force he was to command, the task was already well in hand
under the energetic supervision of Governor-General Lord Lansdowne's military secretary, Lord Melgund (later Governor-General the Earl of Minto). With the assistance of Denison and J.T.
Lambert, an Ottawa lumber agent who negotiated contracts with
shantymen, and with the co-operation of the Canadian government, Melgund was able to have ready for embarkation in less
than a month a contingent of 380 men including a number of
Indians from Quebec and Manitoba. The figure fell short of the
500 hoped for, nor were the men, for the most part, the historic
voyageurs Wolseley remembered. In fact, the vocation had virtually disappeared with improved transportation facilities. But
the Indians had preserved their traditional skills and the shantymen's experience in spring log drives recommended them as
equally serviceable; what they lacked in numbers the men more
than compensated for in zeal. Engaged for six months at $40 per
month, provided with kit and rations, and organized in gangs
under foremen (at $75) whose authority was undoubtedly more
comprehensible to them than Denison's and frequently more respected, it was a 'motley' and, as the *Globe*'s correspondent

noted, sometimes 'well-primed' crew who set sail from Montreal on 14 September bound for Egypt.[39]

In addition to Major Denison, whose appointment as lieutenant-colonel by brevet was confirmed before the *Ocean King* cleared the St. Lawrence, there were five other officers, most of them with experience in managing *voyageurs.* Denison would have preferred for one of them his younger, and inexperienced, brother Egerton. Both Egerton and Septimus Denison had asked for appointments, but for reasons of his own Melgund denied their requests. At his older brother's insistence, Egerton set off for Egypt by himself, determined to find useful employment (he held a captaincy in the British militia) or, if necessary, merely to observe the advance up the Nile. Once in Egypt, however, Egerton was attached to the *voyageur* contingent on Wolseley's order, much to the satisfaction of Fred Denison who desired his brother's companionship and assistance on what was to be a long and lonely campaign in an unfamiliar role. But even before the *Ocean King* had left Canadian waters Denison was wholly preoccupied with his new responsibilities, seeing to the physical, spiritual, and material needs of these rough rivermen who had only a few musical instruments and some table games donated by Lord Lansdowne to occupy them during three weeks of confinement in close quarters.[40] Denison took the difficulties in stride, exerting his authority through a judicious imposition of fines when rough behaviour demanded it, organizing concerts and footraces on deck to keep the men occupied, and conducting weekly interdenominational church services which invariably ended with 'God Save the Queen' in order to 'inoculate the men with a good loyal spirit. ...'[41] By the time the *Ocean King* reached

Alexandria on 7 October, the contingent had settled in to a daily routine that augured well for the journey upriver.

From Alexandria, their route lay along the Nile past Cairo to Assiut, 229 miles by rail, then by steamer to Assuan 300 odd miles farther on, then by rail again for the nine mile journey around the First Cataract, and again by steamer for the last 210 miles to Wady Halfa on the Nubian frontier. The trip upriver took nearly as long as the ocean voyage, nineteen days, but Denison evidently welcomed the leisurely pace which permitted him to visit, and marvel at, the ruined temples of Luxor, Esneh, and Abu Simbel, to collect souvenirs, and to study the climate, geography, and native population of the Nile Valley. On 26 October, a Sunday, the contingent finally reached Wady Halfa and the 'Great Cataract.' Lord Wolseley was impatient, and Denison was ordered to have his men on the river at dawn the following morning.

For the next two months, Colonel Denison and his *voyageurs* had but a single objective: to forward a force of nearly 5,000 men with their arms and supplies, in the whale gigs, from Wady Halfa to Korti, a distance of 330 miles. Instead of encountering three or four major cataracts at predictable intervals along an otherwise navigable river, they discovered a succession of difficult rapids all the way upriver. Through these obstacles they had to track, row, or pole, and occasionally portage, the shallow-drafted gigs weighing a thousand pounds when empty, and nearly three tons with a full complement of men and supplies. Every observer fumbled for words to describe the way in which the men 'unloaded and loaded, rowed and tracked, day by day and hour by hour, under a blazing sun, against that ever-rushing, every changing torrent, between unchanging walls of burning basalt.'[42]

In spite of recurrent attacks of dysentry which daily became more acute, Fred Denison laboured as strenuously as the best of his men passing the whalers up the cataracts. Responsible also for the administrative duties associated with his force, Denison spent much time plying the river in a birchbark canoe issuing directives to foremen, ferrying men to points where they were required, and moving the sick and injured to field hospitals. He also had to settle disputes such as one that arose early in the campaign when some of the men refused to work on the Sabbath. A stern *ultimatum* sent most back to work immediately, and thereafter Denison had few problems except for some of the Winnipeg men, many of whom, the *Globe* reported, were 'bank clerks and law students, etc., mostly athletes' who had volunteered for the sake of adventure.[43] But they soon learned that their commander would not tolerate incompetence. Denison was intent on being with the first elements of Wolseley's force to reach Khartoum. Frequently tackling the most hazardous rapids himself to allay the fears of the soldiers, and to counteract the sometimes too cautious attitude of the regular officers, Denison consistently exposed himself to dangers as great as any encountered by his men. The slow pace of the expedition annoyed him, and his untiring example was perhaps meant to spur on some of his British comrades who evidently did not share his zeal.[44]

With his force concentrated at Korti, on December 27 Wolseley divided his army in two, creating a Desert Column and a River Column; the latter, a 'flying column' with no supply lines, was to continue upriver to clear the Nile, Wolseley's line of communication, of Mahdist partisans. The services of the Canadian *voyageurs* to man the boats carrying the River Column's supplies now became even more vital. But since their contracts would expire just when the River Column was expected to make contact with the Desert Column for the dash on Khartoum early in March, they now had to be re-engaged or sent home. In spite of the generous terms of re-enlistment Colonel Denison offered, including a 50 per cent increase in pay and sight-seeing stopovers in Cairo and London on the return voyage, only 6 foremen and 83 *voyageurs* signed. Thus the majority of the *voyageurs* started downriver on January 20 accompanied by Egerton Denison and one other officer. Fred Denison and the remainder, many of them from the Winnipeg contingent, turned southward with the River Column into the region of the Fourth Cataract, a 'howling waste of granite; a piled-up tangle of desolation.'[45]

Denison had requested to be sent overland with the Desert Column, but Wolseley had refused and, apart from potting away at the crocodiles who infested the Nile above Korti, Denison's excursion into hostile territory was initially uneventful. Later he had all the excitement he might have wished for.[46] Early in February the Mahdists, who had been retreating before the steady advance of the River Column, suddenly regrouped and entrenched themselves on Kirbekan Ridge, a low promontory commanding the Nile gorge that lay ahead of the column. Khartoum had been breached on January 26, Gordon was dead, and the Sudanese now turned on Wolseley's forces with renewed determination. The men in the column perhaps suspected as much, and Colonel Denison had taken to wearing his sword and revolver at all times to be 'on the safe side.'[47]

On the morning of the tenth, the regiments, resplendent in their red battle tunics, stood to arms and then marched off to confront the enemy. The unarmed *voyageurs* were ordered to remain with the boats, but Colonel Denison was attached to the staff of Colonel Alleyne, the assistant adjutant-general and his immediate superior, who commanded the battery of mountain guns positioned in front of Kirbekan Ridge. Thus, Denison had a vantage point from which to observe the battle, although he spent the morning dodging bullets as the Mahdists concentrated their fire on the bombarding British guns. The dervishes, 2000 strong, put up stiff resistance; but they were poorly armed and eventually fled, many being shot as they attempted to swim the river. In all, about 800 lay dead on the field of battle. On the British side, General Earle, two of his staff, and a dozen men were killed, fifty or sixty more wounded. The battle had been Fred Denison's first exposure to fire, and although he 'did not mind ... in the least,' it nevertheless left him wondering if perhaps 'military glory was gained at too great a cost.'[48]

The comment reflected the utterly exhausted condition of Denison and the other Canadians. To their relief, two weeks after this battle Wolseley withdrew his forces from the Sudan, and at the end of February the *voyageurs* began the long journey home. Denison's return, however, was interrupted in Cairo by illness. His condition was diagnosed as acute 'enteric fever' and for the next month he remained in hospital, delirious most of the time, too weak to move or be moved. Finally, in mid-May he was put on board a steamer for England, and, eventually, Quebec.

The Nile Expedition was but a brief interlude in Fred Denison's life, spent for the most part in the shadow of his elder brother George's notoriety as a champion of nationalism and imperialism and as Toronto's most outspoken public man. After his return from Egypt, Fred Denison traded the public's adulation of his part in the expedition for relative obscurity again. He did stand successfully for election to the House of Commons as the member for West Toronto in 1887, a seat he held until his death in 1896 from stomach cancer. But his performance in Ottawa, with the possible exception of his decision to vote with D'Alton McCarthy's 'noble thirteen' over the Jesuit Estates question, was not extraordinary; in fact, there is no record that he ever addressed the House. If obituaries are any measure of a public man's stature, Fred Denison's indicated that although his contemporaries esteemed him as a citizen and friend, they remembered him, because of the Nile expedition, as a soldier of Empire.

Why a quietly successful Canadian lawyer should have thus uprooted himself to participate in an adventure condemned at the time as 'silly quackery'[49] requires an answer as complex, but in many respects as simple, as the character and traditions of the Denison family. Certainly Fred Denison's action was not premised on a desire for military glory, or on a very exact appreciation that Bismarck's map of Europe was being redrawn in Africa. But Toronto, as George Denison was fond of pointing out, was 'the most imperialistic city in the Empire,' and the Denisons had been among Toronto's most ardent advocates of the unity of the Empire for four generations. Imperial citizenship was an extension of their national identity, just as British North America was an extension of the imperial metropolis. In an era when 'imperial unity' had become the fashionable watchword of monarchs and ministers, and in the market place as well, it was inconceivable that the Denisons would do less for the 'dream of the United Empire Loyalists' than familial tradition and their own talents demanded or allowed.

Fred, John, and Septimus Denison, and their younger brother Egerton (1860-1886) who died as the result of fever contracted during military duty in West Africa, made their contribution to the cause of Empire in the form of direct military service. It fell to their elder brother, George Taylor Denison (3rd) to bring together family tradition, history, and the opportunities of the moment in a long, and convincing, defence of the inextricable bond between nation and Empire. His 'struggle for Imperial Unity' was a campaign of thirty years' duration not unlike the Loyalists' attempt to fortify patriotism and to put sedition to rout after the War of 1812. And it earned him, in Victorian Canada, a flattering reputation as 'the Queen's Champion.'

III

'We are a band of brothers'

Confederate song

Professor L.N. Fowler, leading practitioner of the new 'science' of phrenology, attracted the great, those who aspired to fame, and the merely curious to his office on New York's fashionable Broadway. They came, literally, to have their heads examined. Walt Whitman, the poet, was a frequent patron, perhaps to have his 'cosmic consciousness' verified. And George Denison, twenty years old, a Canadian tourist in New York in the autumn of 1859, made the first of several visits hoping to gratify his curiosity about his own future. He was not disappointed. After examining the contours of Denison's skull, Fowler told him that he was industrious, ambitious, 'decidedly wilful,' and of a 'romantic class of mind,' though somewhat lacking in dignity and too stubborn. Moreover, 'your hopes are so strong,' Fowler prognosticated, 'that you will not allow any one to get ahead of you or be more sanguine in their expectations than yourself.' On the strength of that trait, Fowler predicted, Denison would 'yet take

hold of some public enterprize and gain reputation where it requires some uncommon vigour and resolution. ...'[1]

The prediction was precisely what George Denison had hoped
that it might be. A great deal was expected of him, particularly
by his father who once warned him that 'if a man does not make
his mark or be in a fair way of doing it before he is 40 he will
never do anything afterwards.'[2] Twenty years, more than enough
time to realize his potential, lay before him, and he had at his
disposal all of the resources and advantages that being a Denison
conferred. Failure was beyond question.

Born at Rusholme on 31 August 1839, George Taylor Denison's upbringing and education were consistent with familial tradition. He received his formal education at Upper Canada College where he proved to be an indifferent student, invariably
standing well down in the class. But he spent his summers under
the tutelage of his grandfather, Jeremiah Dewson, who taught
him to ride, shoot, and wield a cavalry sabre. In his spare time
he read military history. The heroes of his boyhood were Napo-
leon I and the Duke of Wellington, though he later cast them
aside for Robert E. Lee, the type of man 'that made the anci-
ents believe in demi-gods.'[3] Denison met the general shortly after the Civil War. On his fifteenth birthday, George Denison was
commissioned as an officer in his father's troop. Two years later
he inherited it, as lieutenant and commanding officer. Nearly
six feet tall and a slim 148 pounds, with a shock of dark brown
hair framing a long face dominated by an aquiline nose and an
incipient moustache, Denison looked every inch a 'cavalry swell'
in the cinch-waisted dress uniform of the Dragoons. His trumpe-
ter, unfortunately, was short and fat, and George Denison as

much as any one else recognized the temptation to make 'invidious comparisons' with Don Quixote and Sancho Panza.[4]

After graduation from UCC, Denison had enrolled briefly as a student at Trinity College from which he was expelled in 1858 for being rude to one of the masters. His father attempted to have him reinstated by challenging the competence of the master and the administration, in this case John Strachan, in a diatribe entitled *Trinity College Conducted as a Mere Boy's School, Not as a College* (1858). Strachan, however, refused to be intimidated, and the younger Denison was forced to transfer to the secular University of Toronto, where he received his LL.B in 1861. Three years later he was married to Caroline Macklem, a niece of the Bishop of Niagara and granddaughter of T.C. Street, one of the wealthiest landowners in the Niagara peninsula. Soon they were established in a farm house, 'Heydon Villa,' on his father's estate in West Toronto, yet another addition to the already 'populous colony' of Denisons. Though he rarely confided his innermost thoughts to the diary in which he recorded his activities every day from 1864 until his death in 1925, on his 25th birthday George Denison evidently felt compelled to take stock of his situation. 'I hope that the next twenty five years of my life (if I am spared that long) will be passed as happily as the last,' he wrote. 'It will be the most important epoch of my life. I trust I shall make good use of it.'[5]

Now a lawyer by profession, George Denison nevertheless was utterly uninterested in legal practice. He was a soldier, a cavalry officer by instinct and a military historian by inclination. Both fields offered possible avenues of advancement. His earlier pamphlets on the problems of Canadian defence had been well received, and by 1864 Denison had begun to formulate a reinterpretation of the role of cavalry in modern warfare, based on his observations of the American Civil War. As an officer, his predestined elevation through the ranks of the militia was meteoric. At 28 he was a lieutenant-colonel with aspirations toward a permanent career as a professional soldier. Suddenly, however, his hopes were dashed on the shoals of Canadian politics, and in 1868 he was forced to resign his commission and turn elsewhere to make his mark.

This personal crisis had its origins in the American Civil War. In spite of the official policy of neutrality imposed on British North Americans, young George Denison, like many Upper Canadians, openly supported the Confederacy. His partisanship was motivated by fear that the North's military might would be turned against British North America after the South's defeat, by his empathy with a conservative, agrarian society that he assumed to be not unlike his own, and by the popularized exploits of Confederate cavalry captains who conformed to his conception of chivalric heroes. But all of these reasons paled into insignificance in comparison with the strength of familial tradition, as George Denison (3rd) understood it. The Confederates, after all, were in a position not unlike the Loyalists of Upper Canada for whom life had been a constant struggle to preserve their identity against Yankee aggression. To remind himself continually of the fact, George Denison was a frequent visitor to New Jersey where he thought he had located the tree on which his great-grandfather Lippincott had hanged the rebel Huddy. So strong had Denison's personal antipathy to the United States become, in fact, that when the Toronto City Council moved a resolution expressing sympathy to the people of America after the assassination of Abraham Lincoln in April 1865, the only dissenting vote was a resounding nay from the councilman for St. Patrick's Ward, George Denison (3rd).[6]

In addition, Denison's uncle George Dewson of Florida was a colonel in the Confederate army. Dewson arrived in Toronto in September 1864 under orders from Judah P. Benjamin, Confederate secretary of state, to evaluate potential British North American support for the beleaguered Confederacy.[7] His presence at George Denison's home was an open invitation to the numerous Confederate agents, refugees, and escaped prisoners of war, with whom Toronto abounded, to congregate for entertainment and more serious business. Among the most frequent visitors were Colonel Jacob Thompson, the ranking Confederate commissioner in British North America, his secretary William Cleary, and William 'Larry' McDonald, his transportation agent.

Thompson and Denison soon became constant companions and Denison was admitted to the 'band of brothers' responsible for the raids against Johnson's Island and St. Alban's (Vermont), and the incendiary attack on New York City, in the autumn of 1864. Heydon Villa even became the terminus of the underground railway by which Confederate agents smuggled documents, forwarded by President Jefferson Davis, to the defence counsel for the captured Johnson's Island raiders. Denison's respected name, his position as alderman for St. Patrick's Ward and as a commissioned officer, his relationship to Dewson, and his unabashed zeal for the Confederate cause made him, in Thompson's eyes, a potentially valuable ally. In January 1865 Thompson decided that George Denison was the solution to his most pressing problem.

Early in November 1864 Thompson and McDonald had purchased a steam vessel, the *Georgian*, through one of their operatives, Lewis B. (alias Gervais, John, James T., Dr. James) Bate or Bates, a Mississippian posing as a Saginaw lumber merchant. Their plan was to outfit the *Georgian* as a Great Lakes raider; but no sooner had the vessel cleared Port Colborne, on Lake Erie, for the port of Collingwood on Georgian Bay, than authorities on both sides of the lakes were warned that she was headed for Buffalo to bombard the harbour installations. An armed tug was dispatched to 'make lumber' of the *Georgian*, but its captain, after boarding the vessel and finding the crew drunk (or feigning inebriation), decided she was harmless and permitted her to proceed. Meanwhile, Canadian authorities discovered that a factory in Guelph, Canada West, operated by a cousin of one of the Johnson's Island raiders, was manufacturing shot and shell for a cannon similar to one that had been stolen from the same town. Cannon, munitions, and the *Georgian* all arrived at Collingwood in the week of December 7, and the coincidence was sufficiently remarkable to cause Canadian customs officials to seize the *Georgian* as a suspected privateer. Thompson's only hope of securing the release of the vessel was to sell the *Georgian*, ostensibly at least, to 'some British subject.' Who better than George Taylor Denison?

The transaction was completed on 18 January 1865. A week later, through the influence of one of Denison's political friends, the *Georgian* was released. She never sailed under her new registration. On 7 April 1865 the provincial government again seized the vessel on the strength of information given to David Thurston, United States consul in Toronto, by Godfrey Hyams, a Confederate double agent who claimed that Denison was merely holding the *Georgian* for the Confederacy, and that he and McDonald were altering the vessel's superstructure to accommodate cannons. On board the vessel at Collingwood, the authorities did find Denison and McDonald engaged in suspicious carpentry, and buried under the floor of McDonald's home in Toronto they discovered caches of torpedoes and other munitions.

Vehemently denying the accusations levied against him, Denison petitioned the government to release the vessel and also launched a suit in the Court of Queen's Bench to force the government to show cause for the seizure. There was reason for optimism. After the Confederate surrender on 14 April, most of his Confederate associates returned to the United States. The charges against Denison could not be substantiated as long as Bates, McDonald, Thompson, and Denison's *pro forma* promissory notes, which he had given to Thompson as evidence of the 'sale,' were nowhere to be found. In fact, there seemed to be no one left to dispute the legality of Denison's claim on the vessel. But in December his hopes melted away when David Thurston produced an affidavit signed by Larry McDonald, who was hiding in Kentucky, which undeniably connected Denison with Thompson's clandestine activities. The affidavit persuaded Chief Justice William Draper, in a judgment rendered in March 1866, to deny Denison's suit to recover the *Georgian.* It also cleared the way for David Thurston to proceed with a second suit, initiated in December 1865 on behalf of his government, to recover the vessel for the United States as 'heir-at-law' to Confederate property.

It seemed to Denison that the United States, having crushed the Confederacy, had now declared war on him. Thurston, Denison claimed in a letter to the Toronto *Leader* on 22 January 1866, had even intimated that the renewal of the Reciprocity Treaty of 1854 hinged upon Denison's co-operation in letting the Americans win their case in order to establish a legal precedent, a condition which seemed to place the future commercial prosperity of British North America squarely in Denison's hands. Moreover, it also became apparent that the Attorney-General of Canada, John A. Macdonald, was anxious to facilitate a judgment favourable to the United States, if he was not actually abetting that side. Denison understood that Macdonald's government was prepared to absolve him of any complicity in the *Georgian* affair, and to compensate him for his legal expenses, if he co-operated. Obviously, in the face of such opposition compromise was the best tactic.

As a matter of principle, Denison had no intention of giving up the fight against the United States, particularly in the wake of the Fenian invasions of June 1866. The experience of leading the Governor-General's Body Guard to repel these Irish-American ruffians produced a book, the first copy of which went to United States Secretary of State, William H. Seward, and a strengthened resolve to resist the State Department as vigorously as he had defended the frontier against the Fenians. But as the prospects of winning the battle waned perceptibly in the summer of 1866, Denison decided that if he had to lose the *Georgian* for political reasons, he would have to be compensated. A place in the first parliament of Confederation as the Liberal-Conservative member for West Toronto was his price. The Prime Minister, however, had other plans for the riding, even though it was still a Denison stronghold, and George Denison settled for a promise from Macdonald of an appointment as assistant adjutant-general for cavalry in the new Dominion. The post would assure him a bright future as a career officer.[8] Thus, when the United States won its case in November 1867, George Deni-

51

son was embittered, but not without prospects. After several pointed reminders, Macdonald had promised to take up the question of Denison's promotion with the minister of militia, Sir George Cartier. But by the spring of 1868 Denison still had not received his appointment, and he decided to speak to Cartier personally. During a brief interview in the foyer of the Parliament buildings in April he was informed by Cartier that the government had no intention of gazetting him assistant adjutant-general. Denison resigned his commission on the spot.

The Civil War, the Fenian invasions, and especially the *Georgian* episode confirmed everything that George Denison had been taught, or had observed, about the 'grasping' United States of America, and its treatment of all who abjured the theory and practice of republican democracy. On the other hand, the procrastination and duplicity of Macdonald and Cartier, which Denison regarding as an attempt to 'kick his family out of the party' to which they had been loyal for 75 years,[9] shattered his faith in the Liberal-Conservative party and in Canadian politicians generally. Having declared himself insolvent after nearly two years of continuous litigation, and having resigned his commission, George Denison's prospects of acquiring wealth and reputation either as a soldier or a public man were indeed dim.

Not content to rebuild the faltering law practice which he shared with his younger brother Frederick, Denison turned to the one resource remaining to him. Drawing on his vast knowledge of the military operations of the American Civil War, he produced an iconoclastic re-evaluation of the role of cavalry in modern warfare. But the book, *Modern Cavalry*, published in 1868, fared badly at the hands of English military critics who resented the presumptuousness of this colonial militia officer.

Still, Denison did not have to suffer this last blow to his ego alone. In Ottawa in the spring of 1868 he had become attached to a company of young men who shared his low opinion of Canadian politics and his fear of the United States. And they were equally piqued by the pejorative connotations associated with the term 'colonist' used in reference to a citizen of the new Dominion. Moreover, they were prepared and eager to rectify the situation by shouting aloud the praises of the 'new nationality' embodied in the federal union of British North America.

Denison's circle of new friends consisted of Charles Mair, an ambitious young poet from Perth, Ontario; Henry James Morgan, a federal civil servant and Ottawa *littérateur*; William A. Foster, like Denison a lawyer from Toronto; and Robert Grant Haliburton, secretary of the Nova Scotia Coal Owners' Association and the son of the creator of 'Sam Slick.' These five were in the habit of meeting in Morgan's rooms in the Revere Hotel, after attending the evening sitting of the House of Commons, for 'a smoke and a chat,' though occasionally for somewhat bawdier pursuits.[10] They shared, in particular, a sense of commitment to D'Arcy McGee's vision of a great Canadian political nationality 'bound, like the shield of Achilles, by the blue rim of ocean'; and also a profound respect for the memory of this assassinated 'prophet' of Canada's manifest destiny whose dream, far from being realized, seemed to have been compromised by less far-sighted politicians. The birth of a great nation should constitute the 'noblest period of its history,' Haliburton contended, whereas the Confederation of Canada had created as little patriotic feeling as the incorporation of a 'joint stock company.'[11] To correct this perversion of historical intent, the young men pledged their energies and talents to the promotion of a genuine national sentiment, to the creation of an environment of patriotism, in which men's actions would be dictated by the watchwords 'Canada First.'

Denison and his friends set out initially to define and promote national sentiment in terms of a mythology consistent with their romantic preconception of the nation's destiny. Canadians, Haliburton insisted, were the 'Northmen of the New World,' the descendants of the 'Aryan' races whose superior mentality, institutions, and fighting ability, nurtured by the 'icy bosom of the frozen north,' had allowed them to dominate inferior, especially southern, races. The idea appealed particularly to George Denison who hastened to point out that this geopolitical determinism must eventually be the decisive factor in a 'rattling war' with the United States to assert Canada's independence.[12] These rumblings of aggressive intent were relatively hollow, but nevertheless understandable as a response to the reunified strength of post-war America which appeared to be the chief threat to the success of the Canadian national experiment. But as the subsequent history of the Canada First movement was to demonstrate, the imperialist impulse, defensive or otherwise,[13] could be turned to less laudable ends. In the hands of George Denison and his friends, it soon led to the disruption of national unity.

When, in 1870, the French-speaking Métis of Red River, led by Louis Riel, executed Thomas Scott, an Ontario Orangeman, as a symbolic denial of Ontario's historic territorial and commercial claims in the North West, 'Canada First' became a shibboleth for the narrower imperialism and racialism of Ontario. Guided principally by the jaded opinions about the Métis shared by Mair, who was employed in Red River by the Canadian government, and John Christian Schultz, the intemperate leader of the Canadian party in the colony, Denison and the 'Twelve Apostles,' as the now larger clique secretly styled themselves, galvanized public opinion in Ontario into a bloodthirsty demand for revenge. From April 1870 until the Expeditionary Force reached Red River in July, the Apostles kept Toronto and most of southern Ontario in a constant state of agitation. Using Heydon Villa as their base of operation, they planned and executed demonstrations, supplied the newspapers with inflammatory articles, and generally played on the prejudices of ever susceptible Protestant Ontario. 'Shall French Rebels Rule Our Dominion?' they demanded, consciously implying complicity, or acquiescence, on the part of Macdonald and Cartier. As an indication of the lengths to which the Apostles were prepared to carry their agitation, George Denison even threatened to lead a civil insurrection to save 'half a continent' should Macdonald negotiate with, or pardon, Riel. A thousand miles to the west, Fred Denison, the first member of the force to reach Fort Garry, was raising the Red Ensign over Riel's abandoned headquarters.

The popular response generated by the Apostles' campaign sustained the punitive mentality of the Ontario volunteers serving with the Expeditionary Force as well as the clamour at home for the forcible annexation of the North West Territory to the Dominion of Canada. It also convinced George Denison that a third political party, unencumbered by the bargains and compromises of Confederation, might succeed in Canada. It would be a party 'that would uphold the honour of the Dominion, that would strive to make the name "Canadian" feared and respected; that would look to extending Canada's wealth, strength, and military organization.'[14]

The events of the next two years seemed to affirm Denison's, and the Apostles', distrust of the two old parties. When Sir John A. Macdonald returned from the Treaty of Washington negotiations empty-handed, in spite of his herculean attempt to exact from the United States a commercial treaty favourable to Canada, the Apostles chose to believe, as Denison put it, that Britain, with Macdonald's connivance, had 'huckstered away' Canada's inshore fisheries 'in a disgraceful and humiliating manner.'[15] The apostles thus unwittingly played a role Macdonald had cleverly created for them in order to arouse Canadian national feeling against the treaty. But out of the Apostles' reaction to the treaty, and subsequently to Macdonald's fall from grace after the 'Pacific Scandal' was revealed, emerged the idea for a new departure in Canadian politics. The germ was planted, perhaps, in a pamphlet written in 1871 by W.A. Foster. In *Canada First; or, Our New Nationality*, Foster attempted to envision a Canadian nationality freed from British traditions, 'the mummied idols of a buried past,' and sustained by a nativist impulse rooted in Canada's historical experience. The upshot, he predicted, would be a 'higher order' of national life in which 'purified' patriotism would be the dominant characteristic of political activity. Adding his voice to Foster's, Denison produced a lecture on 'The Duty of Canadians to Canada' in which he carried the implementation of patriotic fervour one step farther, and indeed plotted his own course with the forces of history. Where Canadians demonstrated unpatriotic tendencies, Denison asserted, their fellow citizens ought to 'argue with them quietly, show them the stupidity of their conduct and if they persist in it, brand them as traitors, if not as cowards, point the finger of scorn at them, recognize them not as Canadians.'[16]

The Apostles were thus well along the way toward redefining, from their point of view, a new order of political morality when the 'Pacific Scandal' burst upon the public. George Denison had had the misfortune of again trying to enter politics, this time as an independent Liberal in the riding of Algoma, in the election of 1872 which spawned the scandal. It was rumoured that the Liberal-Conservative 'corruptionists' had spent $6000 to defeat him by 80 votes. The 'Canada Firsters' oft-repeated warning that the older parties were merely 'factions' supporting themselves 'by intrigue, demagogism, and corruption' seemed to have been fully justified.[17] Clearly, it was time for a new broom and, in anticipation of a general election after Macdonald's inevitable demise, the Canada Firsters decided in the autumn of 1873 'to try if a new political party could be made to take hold of public favour – a party that would be more distinctly national if not patriotic than the present ones.' Their first candidate would be Goldwin Smith, the renowned Oxford political economist lately removed to Toronto, who had become the movement's intellec-tual-in-residence.[18] Their first campaign, as it turned out, would be for the West Toronto seat, in a by-election called to test the strength of Alexander Mackenzie's newly formed ministry.

George Denison did not assist at the birth of this new party with its claim to a monopoly on nationalism and patriotism. His friends in Ontario's Liberal government had offered him em-ployment as an immigration commissioner for the province in London, and he was obliged to be out of the country when the Canada First party was launched on 6 December. Before the month was out, however, the Canada Firsters were begging him to return to Canada to rescue their party from annihilation.

Denison subsequently discovered that its first public appearance had been a comedy of errors. At the last moment Smith had decided not to stand for election, and the Canada First party had called a nomination meeting. But the Liberals had packed the hall and had successfully nominated their own candidate, Thomas Moss, to contest the crucial by-election in West Toronto, with a pledge of support from Canada First. Moreover the party's chairman for the meeting had delivered a particularly effete address in which he condemned 'toadyism' to England, thereby leaving the public with the impression that the Canada Firsters were anti-British, for independence, and therefore 'disloyal.' In a final display of their naïveté, the Canada Firsters then published a platform which, in spite of a few planks on the pressing economic problems of the day, was made largely of such abstruse constitutional reforms as the representation of electoral minorities, compulsory voting, and even a federation of Canada and the British West Indies.

The party journals had a field day at Canada First's expense. To the *Globe,* the new party was an 'innocent absurdity.' The Toronto *Sun* described Canada First as a 'wretched abortion' performed by 'a dozen or so briefless lawyers.' Undaunted, in 1874 the Canada Firsters launched their own journal, the *Nation*, and solicited subscriptions to build permanent headquarters for the parent organization of the party, the Canadian National Association. The National Club, on Bay Street, was also incorporated in 1874. But from its inception, as even the most ardent of the Canada Firsters, Foster, was forced to admit, the National Club's success was chiefly attributable to its 'good functions – excellent pub – nice company – best of liquor. ...'[19]

Canada First, as a third political front, was not heard from again. Indeed, it had been stillborn.

George Denison discerned the reasons for Canada First's failure perhaps most clearly. If ever the movement was to be revived, he told Mair in 1876, 'it must be in a new dress, under a new name and in some time of public excitement when some great rallying cry can form a pivot around which the young men can gather.'[20] The Canada First movement, as Denison well knew, had succeeded best in its role as the catalyst of aggressive nationalism. He therefore refused to be associated with the party and its utopian vision of national prestige premised on pristine political behaviour and constitutional purity. But the spirit of Canada First lived on for George Denison, in the memory of the somewhat sophomoric, slightly irresponsible sword rattling of the 'old five of the corner room.'

George Denison nevertheless saw more than the crumbling pretensions of a genuine Canadian nationalist movement amid the ruins of the Canada First party. In a different guise it might well have served as an outlet for his unfulfilled political aspirations. Now nearing middle age, he had become increasingly sensitive about his conspicuous lack of personal achievement. Later, he ascribed his difficulty to the fact that 'the openings for ambition to a Canadian lawyer were not great, the chances of making one's mark very limited.'[21] But the fact remained that he had invested perhaps too much faith in the Liberal party. Before the election of 1872 he had basked in the prospect of acquiring, after a Liberal victory, either the office of Minister of Militia or at least a senior post in the militia. All that could be found for him, however, was the appointment as a provincial immigration commissioner in England. It proved to be an agreeable situation, partly because his duties involved, primarily, what would now be described as 'public relations.' Denison was therefore able to mix business with pleasure since he was obliged to maintain contacts with many prominent upper class Britons and became socially intimate with them. These same men would become valuable allies in his subsequent 'struggle for imperial unity' after 1886 and would ultimately fête him, fifteen years later, as one of the 'staunchest friends of Empire' that Britain ever knew.[22] In the meantime, however, because his appointment was only temporary, Denison was thrown back on his own resources after June 1874. Not surprisingly then, when he heard in 1875 that the Russian government had offered a substantial prize of 5000 *roubles* (about £450) for the best manuscript history of cavalry to be submitted by 1 January 1877, George Denison rose to the challenge. Cavalry history was his forte, and there was yet a reputation to be made as the instigator of a cavalry renaissance.

This, in fact, had been Denison's object in writing his first military work, *Modern Cavalry*. Prior to the American Civil War, it had generally been assumed that the effect of a charge of heavy cavalry, man and horse hurling themselves at the enemy like a projectile, had become obsolete as a tactical weapon given the range and concentration of infantry firepower. On the eve of the Crimean War, a brash young English cavalry officer, Captain Lewis Nolan, had attempted to rescue the *arme blanche* from impending obsolescence by publishing a brilliant, if over-romanticized history of cavalry in which he contended that no European army could withstand a charge of British cavalry. Nolan was the first to fall under the withering fire of the Russian infantry when the Light Brigade rode into the valley at Balaklava. Thereafter, professional soldiers were convinced, as one of them said, that 'the effect of the improved weapons ... on cavalry must be nearly to destroy its utility altogether as an offensive arm on the field of battle.'[23]

Denison disagreed with this assessment largely on the strength of his conversations with eminent Confederate cavalrymen during and after the American Civil War. European soldiers regarded the Civil War as too 'unique' to be a trustworthy primer of new tactics. But the unknown young Canadian militia officer argued in *Modern Cavalry* that the Civil War was worthy of analysis precisely because of the irregular conditions imposed by rifled firearms, topography, and, on the Confederate side at least, the limitations of a citizen army. Far from rendering cavalry obsolete, these conditions had produced a qualitative change in the organization and employment of cavalry which amounted to a revolution in tactics.

The thesis of his book was simple. The raw levies of the Confederate cavalry might be skilled only in horsemanship and the use of arms available to every citizen – rifles, revolvers, and double-barrelled shotguns – but these skills had given it an instant advantage in the early stages of the war. Neither infantry nor cavalry, these troopers were, properly speaking, mounted riflemen capable of performing the duties of light cavalry, for example raiding, scouting, covering a retreat and pursuing a retreating foe, or operating on the flanks of an advancing line as a tactically offensive force. Yet they could also fight dismounted on equal terms with infantry when geography or numbers precluded the use of classical cavalry tactics. In fact, Denison contended, in this latter development lay the real revolution. Trained as infantry, but retaining the instincts and mobility of cavalry, a new force of mounted rifles would combine both speed and concentration of power, the essence of modern strategy. Moreover, being able to confront entrenched infantry with massed firepower, this new arm of the service could adopt defensive tactics within a strategic offensive, another necessity characteristic of modern warfare. Thus organized and employed, cavalry would again become the pivotal arm of the services.

In spite of the fact that Denison had also defended the continued employment of heavy cavalry, armed with the sabre and the lance, when conditions permitted a well-executed charge, British reviewers were not prepared to accept the opinions of a provincial 'yeomanry officer' that cavalry of the line was virtually obsolete, or that the American Civil War, especially the experience of the losing side, was a credible basis for re-evaluating cavalry tactics. Denison refused to recant. Two years later, in 1870, the 'vexed question as to the utility of cavalry of the line in modern warfare' was conclusively settled, at least to Denison's satisfaction, when Prussian infantry armed with breech-loading rifles slaughtered France's chivalry on the field at Sedan.[24]

Thus, when he began to write his essay for the Russian prize in 1875, George Denison's thesis was substantially complete. But he had to write a history of cavalry from biblical times, and the manuscript had to be translated into Russian. It was a time-consuming and expensive task given the paucity of Canadian library resources and the difficulty of obtaining a qualified translator. Eventually, it became evident that Mohammed would have to go to the mountain. Having reactivated his commission in order to appear properly accredited, in the autumn of 1876 Denison set out for London to use the British Museum, then went on to St. Petersburg to work in the Imperial Military Library. On 26 December 1876 he presented his thesis to the prize committee in person. To Denison's astonishment, the committee refused to consider his manuscript. The translation, done by a Russian woman living in New York, was 'far too literal to be either good or pure Russian; ... the phraseology [was] that of a non-Russian, or at least one who was no longer accustomed to think in Russian.'[25] After exchanging a few harsh words with the committee, Denison, physically ill and mentally exhausted, departed for London. There he showed his manuscript to the brothers Macmillan, who published it in English in April 1877 as a *History of Cavalry from the Earliest Times with Lessons for the Future.*

Again, civilian and military reviewers alike refused to be convinced that mounted rifles were a viable tactical weapon at the disposal of modern armies. As late as 1913, when the second edition of *A History of Cavalry* appeared, European soldiers were still debating the merits of cavalry of the line, although Denison's thesis had accurately foreshadowed Boer strategy during the South African War, and the highly mobilized armies of the twentieth century. Strangely enough, when the Russians saw the English version of Denison's manuscript in print they were sufficiently impressed to have it translated and adopted as a compulsory text for the military studies branch of the imperial army. Moreover, General Leontieff wrote to inform Denison in 1877 that he had now been awarded the 5000 *roubles*, 'not as a prize won in a contest, but as very desirable compensation' in consideration of the expense incurred in producing a work of 'incontestably scientific merit.'[26]

Denison was disappointed by the reception accorded to his book, and to some extent by the Russian award since it clearly did not imply the same merit as a fairly won prize. But he had established a reputation as a controversial military historian, and his activities had not gone entirely unnoticed in his own country. In May 1877, Oliver Mowat, premier of Ontario and a personal friend, cabled Denison in London offering him the appointment of police magistrate for the city of Toronto. From Denison's point of view it was an ideal situation. He would be required to work only a few hours a day, leaving ample time for other pursuits, and the salary would be a 'very good addition to his income.'[27] Denison accepted, and for the next 43 years his was the only law that most Torontonians knew.

'The Beak,' as Denison was affectionately known to the court reporters, acquired both reputation and notoriety on the bench. His habit of working for only two hours a day and of clearing the docket in this allotted time (in one instance over 100 cases in 85 minutes) infuriated the City Council who thought their servant should put in a full day's work for a day's pay. A few days of deliberate lethargy, which inevitably created a backlog of cases and a demand from Denison for an assistant magistrate, always brought the councillors to heel. No one was spared the sting of the magistrate's jibes. Court reporters who had the audacity to criticize his methods were often publicly dressed down as 'dewdrops' and 'daisies.' Higher court judges who reversed Denison's decisions on neat points of law, for example that 'beating a drum' and 'playing a drum' were qualitatively different, frequently were the targets of his acerbic castigations. And he was the sworn foe of 'clever and ingenious lawyers' who employed legal technicalities to defeat the ends of 'common sense' justice. In time, Magistrate Denison's court became something of a tourist attraction.

A staunch defender of the punitive nature of the Criminal Code, Magistrate Denison was also a reformer who incurred the wrath of the legal profession when he emerged as the champion of state legal aid to indigents in criminal cases, and to all citizens in civil actions. He liked to boast that, in his court, 'the law was the same for all classes.' But in fact it was not. Magistrate Denison was prepared to tolerate the failings and weaknesses of the masses, yet was intolerant of even minor offences committed by members of his own class who were responsible, he said, by virtue of their superior station, for the maintenance of social stability. That was how Colonel Denison interpreted his own obligation to society, and until 1920 he constituted a one-man 'Vigilante Committee' dispensing, 'as King Solomon did,' justice, not law, to Victorian and Edwardian Toronto.[28]

His position secure, in 1880 George Denison replaced the original Heydon Villa with an imposing, eighteen-room structure situated at the corner of College Street and Dovercourt Road. Its eclectic style reflected the pretensions of the owner, and the Victorian passion for architectural hybridization. A high rectangular brick structure culminating in a New England 'widow's walk,' Heydon Villa's most remarkable adornment was an encircling verandah, built in the style of classical revival, with Grecian porticos and Doric columns. Inside, according to contemporary sketches, imported marble fireplaces, gilt mirrors, and fine carpets were juxtaposed with African spears, hunting trophies, Indian artifacts, and assorted weapons collected from the battlefields of the world, giving the house a charming quality of careful disorder. Here, Colonel George Taylor Denison (3rd), U.E., Magistrate, military historian, and soldier settled into the sort of existence that he had always coveted. He spent his mornings on the bench, and occupied his afternoons in his library, which contained more than 2,000 volumes of military history alone, reading, writing, and keeping up a voluminous correspondence. Evenings were devoted to mess dinners, whist at the National Club, frequent speech-making, and civic functions. For diversion, winter offered a succession of *soirées* appropriate to 'the season'; and summer usually meant a pilgrimage to England where Colonel Denison had cemented lasting friendships with an assortment of public men and some of the nobility during his earlier residence. There was also a cottage in fashionable Muskoka where the family's six children could escape the oppressive heat of Toronto's summers.

But life had its darker side as well. Suddenly and tragically Carrie Denison died on 26 February 1885, victim of an illness of which she had supposedly been cured eight years before. Then, before George Denison and his children could recover from this domestic tragedy, he was ordered to go to war. Leaving his children in the care of his sister-in-law, Julia, whose husband was with the British army in Egypt, on 2 April George Denison embarked for the North West where Louis Riel had once again challenged the authority of Sir John A. Macdonald's government. Quite apart from the fact that Denison's military obligations complicated his domestic life at a most inopportune moment, he had little enough sympathy for the government's cause in any case. Defence against the Fenians in 1866 had been a 'holy war,' but now the 'warlike enthusiasm' of the Canadian militia would be used to protect what was, in his opinion, 'a Govt. of land sharks that have villainously wronged the poor native and the ... settler.' A just war to defend or acquire territory was one thing; but it was 'a poor quarrel to make the best of it' in which

Indians and Métis became the scapegoats of a government that had 'humbugged the public' more times than enough.[29] Nevertheless, Denison and the 75 officers and men of the Body Guard who accompanied him did their duty, even though it involved them primarily in escort duty far from the action. General Middleton, the commanding officer, evidently had not read Denison's book on the proper employment of cavalry.

After his return to civilian life Denison plunged into his work at the police court, and into the task of trying to raise his family alone. Still, there was time enough for his habitual pastimes, including a holiday in England on the occasion of Queen Victoria's Golden Jubilee in 1887 as the guest of Lord Wolseley. Colonel Denison also found time to court Helen Amanda Mair, a niece of his old friend Charles Mair, and twenty years his junior. They were married on 1 December 1887, and after a honeymoon in the southern states where they were the guests of the governor of Virginia, Fitzhugh Lee, they returned to 'the gayest winter that Toronto [had] ever seen.'[30]

IV

'The Queen's champion'

For more than a decade, since his defeat in the 1872 general election and the subsequent demise of Canada First, George Denison had remained, somewhat unhappily, apolitical. His role as a public servant permitted him to be gratuitously so in any case. At least, Denison was able to rationalize his situation by claiming that the public's trust in their magistrate resided in his strict objectivity on all questions. Nevertheless, at heart George Denison was a born partisan, not for any political faction, but for the cause of nationality which Canada First had been forced to abandon so peremptorily after 1873. Nor was it conceivable that a man whose entire life since adolescence had been devoted to a quest for either fame or notoriety as a public man would have been content to lay his ambitions to rest under the robes of a stipendiary magistrate. In fact, the old ambitions, the products of family tradition and parental expectations, remained. All he required was a cause.

The opportunity finally presented itself in 1886-1887 with the appearance of the Commercial Union movement, a scheme devised by two or three American entrepreneurs to promote the creation of a North American free trade area and, consequently, continental prosperity amid general economic depression. To some Canadians the movement smacked of yet another American threat to the economic and political integrity of the Dominion. 'I have always preached it to our people,' Denison explained in a letter to author William Kirby, 'that the Yankees are our greatest if not only enemies and that we should never trust them.'[1] It was time for a 'rattling war,' of words at least, and his own course was eminently clear.

Ironically, perhaps, it was the response of people like George Denison which invested 'Commercial Union' with much of its emotional capital. The Conservative party ignored it. The Liberals, anxious to strike for a 'bold policy' which would lead them out of the wilderness of opposition, considered Commercial Union, then opted for 'Unrestricted Reciprocity,' since the idea of commercial unity suggested overtones of political continentalism. On the other hand, Farmers' Institutes across southern Ontario generally supported the movement, as did a number of prominent individuals. Among the latter the most notable was Goldwin Smith. An anti-imperialist and one of the brahmins of the 'Manchester School' of economists, Smith had long been an advocate of the annexation of Canada to the United States. He regarded this development as inevitable on the assumption that Canadian nationhood, the product of British anti-imperial policies, was destined to fail with the atrophy of the British Empire. But apart from Smith's intellectual commitment to conti-

nentalism, Commercial Union had no strong champions and few
converts when Colonel Denison set out deliberately to use this
'widespread conspiracy ... fed with ... Yankee money' as the
agent provocateur of national unity.[2]

Instinctively, Colonel Denison would have done everything in
his power to combat what he regarded as American aggression
in any case, a well-known trait which his opponents subsequently played upon to discredit him as a fanatical alarmist. But
on this occasion he had no intention of fighting continentalism
merely to gratify his own prejudices. He and Mair agreed that
nothing had been done to promote national unity since the demise of Canada First. 'If such a thought were not too sangui-
nary,' Mair complained in 1888, 'I almost wish the Yankees
would attack us.'[3] Indirectly, with the appearance of Commercial Union, the attack had been made. Presented with the issue
and the climate necessary to resurrect the spirit of Canada First
'in a new dress' and to strike a blow for patriotism, Colonel
Denison would not let the opportunity pass. Far from being
merely an alarmist, he privately welcomed with boyish enthusiasm each new expression of Yankee 'crooked work.' After
President Cleveland's 'Retaliation Message' of 1888, Denison
confided to Kirby: '... if only we are so fortunate as to have
Cleveland press the matter to the end, it will create a magnifi-
cent national spirit. For the first time in a long while, I have
great hope for our future.'[4]

In Denison's opinion, it was not enough, however, merely to
confront continentalism with patriotism. To orient national sentiment in a positive direction both a political and an emotional
counterweight to continentalism were required. He discovered
his 'antidote' in the Imperial Federation League. Founded in

Britain in 1884, the League's objective was to promote the consolidation of the resources, chiefly military, of the existing empire as an agent of British supremacy amid the resurgence of European imperial rivalry. By preaching the mutual benefits of an imperial political federation in which the colonies would be given a voice at Westminster in return for contributions to imperial defence, the League hoped to reconcile the mother country and the self-governing dominions after half a century of estrangement. Canadians, however, were uninterested in any scheme likely to jeopardize the growth of dominion autonomy, and although a Canadian branch of the League was formed in 1885, it attracted few proselytes prior to 1887. But Colonel Denison saw in the Imperial Federation movement a useful alternative to continentalism. The idea of 'imperial unity' conjured up in his mind a sense of identification between the present 'crisis' and a historical past in which Canadians, offered a choice between 'loyalty' and imperial disintegration, had defended the 'unity of the Empire.' Similarly, the sentimental associations evoked by the 'British connection,' and the pride in Empire generated by the new imperialism, contributed to the potential appeal of Imperial Federation as an antidote to continental union.

Conversely, Denison suffered no illusions that the Imperial Federation movement could be anything but a means of combatting the 'd___d fools' who flirted with Commercial Union, Unrestricted Reciprocity, and annexation. Canadians would never sacrifice their independence to the cause of imperialism, and therefore the movement would have to be defined in terms acceptable to Canadians, in terms of a 'federation of strict equality.' Thus, when the Toronto branch of the League was formed on 24 March 1888 for the purpose of combatting the 'treason-

71

able conspiracy' of the continentalists, Colonel Denison left no one in doubt as to the new meaning and purpose of Imperial Federation. Henceforward the object of the League in Canada would be to promote imperial unity only through a system of imperial tariff preferences designed to foster increased inter-imperial trade as an alternative to continentalism. This new arrangement would contribute to the prosperity and security of the Empire as a whole and equally of its parts, but specifically it would strengthen the bonds between Canada and the mother country, to the mutual advantage of both. A positive step in the direction of imperial unity would be taken, but without detriment to dominion autonomy, and Canada, both politically and commercially, would be preserved from the 'grasping and aggressive' designs of the United States of America. 'Such a scheme,' Denison speculated, 'would knock the Yankees silly.'[5]

Denison launched his double-barrelled campaign to promote loyalty to Canada and the Empire, and to expose the treasonable designs of the continentalists, in 1888. As chairman of the national organizing committee of the Imperial Federation League and vice-president of the Toronto branch, he was largely responsible for the tremendous growth of the movement in Canada. Where only four local branches of the League had existed in 1886, on the eve of the election of 1891 there were 31 branches representing every major centre of population from Halifax to Victoria. In the Toronto branch alone membership rose from less than 300 to more than 750 in the same period. By November 1889 Denison had written so many letters, reports, speeches, and articles in support of the movement and against the conspirators that he had begun to experience severe pains in his writing arm; his doctor forbade him to write for three months in order to ward off chronic writer's cramp. But he could still talk, and the Colonel was at his best on the platform in front of a large, appreciative (i.e., 'loyal') audience. Equipped with a reproduction of a map, originally printed by the New York *World*, showing the 'Future Great Republic' with 27 additional states carved out of Canada, he would tell his audience that the Commercial Union movement was a scheme devised by the United States to 'annihilate' Canada, just as it had annexed Louisiana, Texas, California, Florida, and Alaska. Each day brought fresh evidence of American intentions, and Canadians soon might have to resort to arms to defend themselves not only against American invaders but also against Canadian 'renegades' since the movement 'originated in treason' – Erastus Wiman, a Canadian expatriate living in New York, was one of the founders of Commercial Union. Canada's one salvation, Denison would tell his audience, its one hope of thwarting both the Commercial Unionists and the Liberal party, was Imperial Federation which guaranteed Canadians virtual independence, indeed a 'splendid isolation' enforced by the greatest military power in the world. In return, Canada had only to abandon the 'National Policy' of protection in favour of a system of imperial preferences as a contribution to imperial consolidation.

Denison was not allowed to go unchallenged. The Liberal journals especially disliked his habit of equating Commercial Union and their party's policy of Unrestricted Reciprocity; but they also berated his 'loyalism,' his enthusiasm for the imperial idea, and his incessant sword-rattling. 'It is a grand thing,' ran one *Globe* lampoon, '... to have at least one patriot always in a humour to make mincemeat of the couple of million blue-coated troops that Brother Jonathan [now Uncle Sam] could put into

73

the field.' In a more serious vein, the *Globe* ventured to suggest that Denison the 'Imperialist' was equally a 'traitor' to the cause of Canadian nationalism.[6] The Colonel willingly accepted being constantly 'abused, attacked, threatened and ridiculed,' in return for the privilege of using the newspapers as a public forum; in fact, he began to evaluate the success of his forays on the strength of newspaper reaction.

New branches of the League, meetings of national and benevolent societies and lodges, mess dinners, national holiday celebrations, civic functions, and school prize days were all convenient vehicles for Denison's propaganda. Neither the very old nor the very young were spared. At the beginning of the fall school term in 1890, the Toronto *Empire*, a Conservative paper and Denison's only journalistic ally, was induced to sponsor a school essay contest on the subject of 'The Patriotic Influence of Raising the Flag over School Houses.' The prize for the best essay from each Ontario county was a Red Ensign measuring twelve feet by six feet. Colonel Denison not only acted as sole judge for the contest, but compiled a collection of predominantly Loyalist verse entitled *'Raise the Flag,' and Other Patriotic Songs and Poems* to be used as both secondary prizes and source material. Four thousand copies of the book were distributed to Ontario school children, teachers, and school officials. Moreover, the League also secured an Ontario Department of Education ruling that the Red Ensign had to be flown over schools on the anniversaries of Canadian-American battles, such as Queenston Heights. Equally anxious to give the children's fathers an 'education in loyalty,' Denison then attempted to have Sir John A. Macdonald call out the rural militia corps, several thousand strong, for a few weeks of drill under arms in the spring of 1890. But Macdonald was not as convinced as Denison that the next election would be fought on the issue of 'loyalty *versus* disloyalty,' and he therefore declined to subject the electorate to this lesson in patriotic duty.[7]

So confident was Macdonald of his hold on the electorate that in January of 1891 he asked for a dissolution and an election on the strength of a well-founded assumption that his government would soon conclude a reciprocity treaty with the United States. He would steal a march on Liberals, Commercial Unionists, and Imperial Federationists alike. To his chagrin, however, the American Secretary of State, James Blaine, who had hinted before the dissolution at the strong possibility of negotiations, subsequently denied publicly that his government had any intention of discussing such a treaty. Faced with an election, and robbed of the means of victory, Macdonald turned, ironically, to the 'loyalty issue' that Denison and his cohorts had kept alive and burning for three years. When Macdonald then attacked the 'veiled treason' of Unrestricted Reciprocity and Commercial Union, and invoked the British connection, he was preaching to the converted. The Conservatives won the election, but Colonel Denison was convinced that a still greater battle lay ahead.

Denison's pessimism, in spite of the undeniable success of his three years' campaign, was prompted primarily by his growing obsession with the 'disloyalty' of Professor Goldwin Smith. Friends for many years, Smith and Denison had customarily respected each other's right to hold dissenting opinions about the path of Canadian development. But after 1886, as Goldwin Smith increasingly identified with the aspirations of the continentalists, Colonel Denison found it more and more difficult to abide, as he would have it, Smith's attempt 'to play the part of a second Tom Paine in a new revolution.'[8] To a considerable degree, Denison's animosity arose out of a series of lectures on 'Loyalty,' 'Aristocracy,' and 'Jingoism' which Smith delivered to the Young Men's Liberal Club of Toronto in the winter of 1890-1891 at the height of the 'loyalty crisis.' Billed as Smith's 'last public utterance' on the question of Canada's political destiny, the lectures attacked the agents, as Smith saw them, of Canada's continued colonial status. Without naming Denison directly, Smith belaboured the 'loyalists' whose veneration of dead institutions, ideals, and ancestors had become the basis for their aristocratic pretensions, and for a *noblesse oblige* school of patriotism in Canada. These 'jingoes,' Smith protested, had turned public schools 'into seedplots of international enmity,' and 'indulged in insolence towards ... fellow citizens' with impunity. They might soon claim the right to sabre dissenters on the street, all in the name of loyalty. Apologizing to those whose patriotism was genuine, Smith concluded that anyone who required 'the hoisting of flags, chanting of martial songs and the celebration of battle anniversaries' as patriotic stimulants 'must be sick.'[9]

Smith's lectures firmly convinced Denison that the professor was a 'disloyal poltroon' whose 'presence in Canada was a source of regret to the whole population,'[10] a conclusion which seemed justified, in Denison's opinion, by Smith's activities in the wake of the 1891 election. Within six months of the defeat of Unrestricted Reciprocity at the polls, 'Continental Unity' clubs began to make their appearance in southern Ontario, and within a year a province-wide Continental Unity Association had been formed with Goldwin Smith as honorary provincial president. Simultaneously, a group of wealthy American entrepreneurs created the Continental Union League in New York with the object of bludgeoning Canada into commercial union by lobbying for more stringent American protectionist tariffs. A spy, 'Marcus R.,' who was paid out of Canadian Customs Department funds, provided the Conservative party with a constant stream of pilfered documents relating to the Continental Union League's activities. David Creighton, editor of the *Empire* and the spy's Toronto contact, forwarded copies of the documents to Denison. They suggested, without offering incontrovertible proof, that Smith had been encouraging the Continental Union League to support regional independence movements in Canada as an alternative to action at the level of national politics.

This evidence was all that Colonel Denison needed to make Goldwin Smith the whipping boy in a final display of patriotic zeal. In rapid succession, Denison had Smith drummed out of the prestigious Anglo-Canadian St. George's Society, barred from Upper Canada College's prize days (Smith had for many years awarded the prize in Classics), and virtually ostracized from polite society. Finally, in 1896, by threatening to have his own name struck from the role of graduates, Denison was able to prevent the University of Toronto from conferring on Smith a degree *honoris causa* in recognition of his contribution to the intellectual life of Toronto. Denison failed in a further attempt to curb Smith's activities by requesting that Toronto newspapers refuse him space in which to reply to his tormentors. Denison contended that circumscribing Smith's freedom of speech would be a relatively painless method of curtailing his 'treasonable' utterances. In France, Denison pointed out to editors, Smith 'would have been consigned to the same convict settlement as the traitor Dreyfus,' and probably would have been lynched in his beloved United States.[11]

The destruction of Goldwin Smith wrote an end to one aspect of the campaign instigated by Denison in 1888. What had begun as a rationally conceived scheme to play off loyalty to the Empire against continentalism in order to promote national unity and patriotism, had become a vendetta between two equally doughty champions of antithetical concepts of national destiny. 'Loyalty' appeared to have triumphed, but perhaps only because in this instance the sword had proved more durable, if less incisive, than the pen.

The other aspect of Denison's campaign, the commercial and political objectives embodied in the Imperial Federation movement in Canada, had been less fruitful than the chauvinistic experience for which the League had served as a vehicle. The imperial federationists in England, free traders for the most part, were openly hostile to the concept of imperial trade preferences. In an 1892 report to the British government outlining the principles of imperial federation, they relegated imperial preferential trade to last place among the 'non-essential' measures which might be conducive to imperial consolidation. But they dwelt at length on the immediate necessity of increased dominion fiscal responsibility for the defence of the Empire. The Canadian League, with support from the moderate fair-trade wing of the parent organization, tried to modify the report's insistence on unity-for-defence as the primary objective of imperial federation, but without success. The defence faction controlled the executive committees of the parent league. They paid a heavy price, however, for their high-handed treatment of the Canadian League, of which Colonel Denison became president in 1893, for without the support of the senior dominions the British League could not pretend to speak for the Empire. When Sir Charles Tupper, on behalf of the Canadian League, publicly rejected unity-for-defence as the essential basis of imperial federation, the League took the only course compatible with the apparent ideological rift and dissolved in the summer of 1893.[12]

Dissolution proved to be merely a signal for the warring factions to regroup their forces. The unity-for-defence group immediately reconstituted themselves as the Imperial Federation (Defence) Committee. In response, the moderates of the defunct parent organization entered into negotiations with Colonel Denison's League and out of their discussions emerged a new organization in 1896, the British Empire League. In every respect, the objectives of the new League reflected the influence of its Canadian co-sponsors. Unity-for-trade was erected as the primary function of imperial co-operation; and the League's program acquired an almost mercantilistic caste in its insistence that the safety of the Empire resided solely in the creation of an inter-imperial trading area protected not only by tariffs but by the Royal Navy. Colonel Denison argued, however, that England 'was not safe while she is dependent for her ... life ... upon the mercy of ... nations ... hostile to us. ... If England was starved into submission, the outlying colonies would be involved in the common ruin. ...'[13] At a single stroke, apparently, the British Empire League's policy offered to resolve the problems of Empire by exchanging colonial trade for British protection, not a new, but definitely a contentious solution.

The years 1896-1899 were halcyon days for George Denison and his band of three hundred or so 'imperialists' who, in spite of their decimated ranks, boasted the leadership of such energetic public men as Sir Charles Tupper, Sir Sandford Fleming, George M. Grant, and George Parkin. They rarely agreed among themselves, a wide gulf separating Tupper the stubborn nationalist and Parkin the *civis imperium*, Grant the cool intellectual and Denison the headstrong man of action. But out of their diverse talents and biases sprang the momentum which propelled the cause of imperial unity forward in Canada, a cause that fed eagerly on every change in the fortunes of Empire. When the new Liberal government of Wilfrid Laurier, with whom Denison became the best of friends and, later, the worst of enemies, offered Britain preferential tariff considerations in 1897, Colonel Denison and the British Empire League required no further proof that Canada had moved into the vanguard in the struggle for imperial unity. They redoubled their efforts to accelerate the process. Coincidentally, Denison's friend and correspondent, Lord Salisbury, whom he had first met during a visit to England in 1890, had returned to power in 1895 at the head of a Unionist government that included Joseph Chamberlain, the most outspoken of Britain's new imperialists, as colonial secretary. Chamberlain's infectious imperialism fired Canadian imperialists with visions of a glorious destiny. They could not yet support his formula of co-operation for imperial defence in return for consultation through a 'Great Council' of the Empire as the new basis of imperial federation, but clearly they were impressed by Chamberlain's rhetoric, just as he was encouraged by the existence of the League in Canada and its effective work. Finally, after the dark days of the Venezuelan crisis of 1895, the prospect of an incipient Anglo-American *rapprochement* paved the way for a semblance of harmony in Canadian-American relations as well. Colonel Denison of all people was even prepared 'to speak quite friendly of the United States' if an Anglo-American *détente* would free Canadians to pursue the interests of nation and Empire uninhibited by past tensions.[14] All signs, especially the effusion of imperial sentiment connected with Queen Victoria's Jubilee celebrations in 1897, which Denison attended, seemed to point to an early redefinition of the imperial relationship compatible with Canadian interests.

For Colonel Denison, this spirit of optimism was short-lived. The international crises of 1898, Fashoda and the scramble for commercial and strategic hegemony in China, planted nagging doubts in his mind about Great Britain's continued imperial supremacy. Also, the emergence of the United States as an imperialist power, symbolized by the Spanish-American War and the ruthless suppression of the Philippines, gave rise to renewed concern for the defensive cement of Empire. 'Spain has been taught that might prevails,' Denison observed, and, with the 'American mob' in an expansionist mood, he considered that Canada might well be the next victim.[15] Given her inadequate defences, Canada's security resided squarely with the military and naval strength of the Empire. By the spring of 1899, then, Colonel Denison had begun to question seriously the League's existing program for imperial consolidation. He was on the brink of accepting the necessity of limited colonial contributions to imperial defence when the Boer War pushed him, irrevocably, across the threshold of jingoism.

Denison's 'imperialism' came full circle with the outbreak of war in South Africa. The 'thrill' of admiration he experienced at seeing the 'best blood' of the Empire shed 'to uphold the rights of one or two hundred thousand ... fellow colonists,'[16] derived from that emotional pride in Empire which sustained the aggressive nationalism of Britons in the age of imperialism. It was the sentiment to which Chamberlain had appealed in 1897 when he envisioned the day that colonial troops would 'share in the dangers and glories' of imperial military ventures. Now Colonel Denison had become Chamberlain's disciple, and he was ready to advocate imperial responsibilities for Canada not merely to promote Canadian security, but to garner for Canada the prestige, the rewards, the power associated with the idea of Empire. Thus, Denison was among the first to demand full Canadian participation in the war. 'We have been children long enough,' he told a meeting of fellow officers; 'let us show the Empire that we have grown to manhood.'[17]

Privately, Laurier begged Denison 'not to make a fuss' over the government's decision not to contribute an official contingent of Canadian troops to the war effort. 'All our conceptions of England's power were wrong,' he suggested to Denison, if Britain could not win this 'little war' herself.[18] Denison immediately divined the root of Laurier's cautious attitude. The prime minister was chary of the effect which the militarism of too zealous friends of the Empire would have in Quebec where opposition to Canadian participation in this imperialist war was gaining steady momentum. Colonel Denison chose to equate French Canada's nationalism with racialism, and race, as he tried to explain to Laurier, had nothing to do with loyalty. If imperial unity, as a safeguard against aggression, was a 'good thing' for English Canada, it must be good for Quebec as well and therefore, Denison replied, all who dissented, especially the ultranationalist Henri Bourassa, must be disloyal. On that note, Denison's brief honeymoon with Sir Wilfrid Laurier came to an abrupt end. As a contemporary Parisian observed, more than the threat to Empire posed by the Boers it was the 'marked coldness of ... Quebec' to imperialism which fired the 'patriotic frenzy' of people such as Colonel Denison.[19]

In keeping with his new posture, it was imperative for Colonel Denison and the British Empire League in Canada to persuade public opinion to accept more responsibility for the military strength of the Empire. Denison now asked Canadians to pay for garrisoning Royal Naval installations in Canada in order to relieve Britain of the expense, for creating a Canadian naval reserve, and, eventually, for building Canadian warships to serve with imperial forces. He also supported the idea of making annual payments to the Royal Navy calculated on the yearly Canadian commercial tonnage it protected. His most radical departure, however, was the concept of a *Kriegsverein*, an imperial war-chest administered jointly by Great Britain and the Dominions, to be raised through the imposition of a five or ten per cent duty on all non-imperial goods entering imperial ports. Foreign nations would underwrite the military supremacy of the British Empire, paying the price of exclusion from the Anglo-Saxon club.

What appealed most to Denison about this latter scheme was that the Dominions could contribute to imperial defence at no cost to the colonial taxpayer. He had always equated their reluctance to accept new imperial responsibilities with the expense involved. He also believed that the lack of enthusiasm for the cause of Empire among its non-Anglo-Saxon 'alien' population could be overcome by a scheme which clearly demonstrated that 'loyalty' cost nothing yet reaped material benefits. Denison did not pause to weigh the cost of the scheme in constitutional terms. He was already committed to the idea that the defence of the Empire was a responsibility which Canada must accept willy-nilly, and there could be no looking backward.

Denison realized that the critical stumbling block for his plan lay in the impasse between British free traders, who would not sacrifice their economic principles to the cause of imperial unification, and colonial nationalists who refused to subordinate their autonomy in order to accept imperial responsibilities. His strategy therefore consisted of one final attempt to bring the two factions together by massing public support for his and the Canadian League's scheme on the eve of the colonial conference of 1902. In April he embarked for England to spend two months proselytizing for the *Kriegsverein* idea with a view to evoking such a public demand for acceptance that there would be no possibility of the outcome being ruined 'by sloth, or apathy, or stupidity.'[20]

Denison had been forewarned by the parent League that this was a dangerous tack to pursue since his proposal was an issue that could 'rend the country from top to bottom';[21] and when he persisted, the British Empire League in the United Kingdom refused to endorse his campaign. But he insisted that the free traders were in the minority and not representative of British public opinion. For the next two months, over the length and breadth of the British Isles, he argued the merits of his plan which offered markets for the colonies, self-sufficiency for Great Britain, and collective security against the Empire's imperialistic rivals. In Bristol, Paisley, Glasgow, Tunbridge Wells, Liverpool, Edinburgh, and London he attacked the evils of free trade. The system ought to be abolished, Denison contended, because Britons in effect were trading with the enemy and planting the seeds of their own destruction.

Invariably there were rumblings of objection and dissent, not the least of which emanated from those who objected to Denison's claim that he represented the opinion of the majority of Canadians. No sooner had Laurier and his delegation arrived in Britain for the forthcoming conference than the press was hastily summoned by Dr. Frederick Borden, Laurier's minister of militia, who informed British journalists that Denison spoke neither for the government nor for the people of Canada. As a result, Denison was forced to admit publicly that he spoke only for the British Empire League in Canada on the issues to be debated at the colonial conference. With that, the British press concluded that he had 'said too much' either to be a credible barometer of imperial sentiment in Canada or to have any influence on the outcome of the conference. 'I tried to do my best,' Denison half-apologized to the Canadian League; '... if our position is sound it will force its way in spite of mediocre village politicians who ... muddle things when they interfere.'[22]

The ensuing colonial conference thoroughly justified all of Colonel Denison's earlier misgivings. Laurier and his ministers refused to discuss any scheme of imperial consolidation which might tend toward increased imperial centralization, in spite of the efforts of Chamberlain and the Admiralty to persuade them otherwise. The conference therefore dealt a death blow to the *Kriegsverein* and *Zollverein* concepts, and to Chamberlain's vision of a genuine 'imperial federation' which would become the constitutional medium of dominion responsibility for imperial defence. In the end, reciprocal preferential trade and continued conferences stood alone as the broadest immediate degree of imperial co-operation acceptable to the majority of imperial statesmen. Colonel Denison could only conclude that the 'disintegrating influences' had triumphed, and that the cause of imperial consolidation was, for the moment, lost. Imperial security now had become a question, he lamented to Sir Sandford Fleming, of *'sauve qui peut.'*[23]

In the wake of the colonial conference of 1902, Colonel Denison quietly abandoned the fight. He was powerless to do more for imperial unity while Laurier remained in power and the free traders held the upper hand in England. Privately, Denison maintained that Britain was a 'nation of idiots' ruled by 'idiots' who deserved whatever fate held in store for them if they persisted in their free trade heresy. Canada would survive, in the meantime, on the strength of her burgeoning wheat economy which had emasculated, temporarily, the attractions of continentalism, and kept the Liberals 'loyal' at least for the time being. Satisfied that he could do no more, Colonel Denison retired from the fray to write his 'political reminiscences,' *The Struggle for Imperial Unity.*

Denison's role in the struggle scarcely needed chronicling, since it was recognized by friend and foe alike. The Earl of Minto wrote to him in October 1903 offering to recommend him for a C.M.G. as a reward for his efforts; and a year later Lord Dundonald, the general officer commanding, proposed to nominate him for an imperial military decoration in recognition of his services to the Canadian militia and the Empire. Denison declined both honours as being too little, too late, given his youthful desire for recognition, and also because he feared that his sincerity of purpose might be compromised in the public mind if he accepted. One who never doubted Denison's sincerity was Henri Bourassa. The French-Canadian nationalist paid tribute to the Colonel as a 'brave and straightforward' imperialist; but for that reason, he added, 'I fight you as an "enemy" of Canada.'[24] This description of himself must have struck Colonel Denison as being inordinately unfair, particularly since he was fond of comparing himself to Schiller's legendary Swiss patriots who sanctified their uncompromising nationalism with the oath on the Rütli: *'Wir wollen sein ein einig Volk von Brüdern ...* we wish to be one single nation of brothers.' For his part, Colonel Denison could not comprehend Bourassa's 'Little Canadianism,' the inability to reconcile imperial unity and the existence of a Canadian political nationality. *The Struggle for Imperial Unity*, published in 1909, attempted to demonstrate that the two were inseparable.

As do most of Denison's published works, *The Struggle for Imperial Unity* makes it clear that the 'dream of the United Empire Loyalists' gave form and substance to George Denison's concept of nationality. Canadian nationhood, as Denison understood it, was above all else a response to the threat of imperial disintegration posed by the American Revolution. The Loyalists' desire to maintain the 'unity of the Empire' and to preserve their own identity as *British* North Americans had provided the initial impetus and determination which led to the creation of a distinctly British nation in northern North America. The idea of 'imperial unity,' Denison argued, was therefore essentially North American in origin, Canadian in origin, and quite inseparable from the other national objectives of Canadians, the more so because the Loyalists' experience had been repeatedly reinforced by the experience of subsequent generations of Canadians. The regularly recurring necessity of having to defend the 'dream of the United Empire Loyalists' against the aggressive imperialism of the United States of America was, for George Denison, the one constant theme in Canadian history, and the ultimate catalyst of Canadian nationalism. In the memory and the symbolism of these confrontations, and in the knowledge that they would be repeated in future, lay the roots of a vigorous national sentiment, a defensively imperialistic sentiment around which all Canadians could unite, as the Loyalists had, to assert their special identity in North America and to promote their destiny in spite of the United States. In this struggle, it was the unity and the power of the Empire that gave Canadian nationalism a decisive advantage. As a more recent writer has remarked: 'The British Empire belonged to Canadians, the power it represented was rightly theirs to share, because of the sacrifices of the loyalists. Animated by this vision, the loyalist descendants and those who regarded the United Empire Loyalists as the founders of the nation looked forward to the steady extension of Canadian authority until it overshadowed the power of the republic from which their ancestors had fled. In the loyalist tradition imperialism was a form of redemption.'[25] Perhaps more than any other public man of his generation, George Denison personified this peculiarly loyalist mix of imperialism, nationalism, and anti-Americanism which promised to propel Canada forward in an heroic struggle for survival.

Colonel Denison's response to Laurier's proposed reciprocity agreement with the United States, announced early in 1911, was predictable. 'Laurier & Fielding have made a great mistake,' he advised Austen Chamberlain in March; 'they did not reckon on the innate hostility of the Canadians to the United States – the result of 100 years of ill treatment and trickery.'[26] Privately, Denison begged Laurier and Fielding, the minister of finance, to abandon the agreement lest they fall into the sins of 1887 and victim to a 'conspiracy' contrived by the enemies of Canada and of the Empire. But, on the other hand, he foresaw the possibility, if the Liberals pressed the reciprocity issue, of yet another confrontation between nationalism and continentalism which might, at long last, evoke a ringing assertion of national unity. As he told Mair, they might yet live to witness the triumph of the principles of 'Canada First,' sufficient pretext for Denison to work as hard as anyone in Toronto to defeat reciprocity and its supporters. By his own estimation, copies of chapter XII of *The Struggle for Imperial Unity*, describing the Liberals' earlier 'treason,' found their way in broadsheet or editorial form into not less than twenty thousand homes; and the Colonel again mounted the platform to preach the power of patriotism. The battle raged from March until 21 September when the electorate went to the polls to administer a crushing defeat to the Liberal party. Colonel Denison was moved to expressions of unbounded elation. 'Glory Hallelujah!' he shouted. The struggle that had begun in 1776 had ended, and in such a glorious fashion. 'Uncle Sam' at last had been delivered 'a damned good kick.'[27] The Colonel's only remaining ambition was to see the British Empire permanently united.

As it happened, the election of 1911 was George Denison's last public campaign. He did not fade into obscurity by any means, for at 72 he was as vigorous as he had been at 40. But after the 1911 election questions of imperial unity and of American domination began to lose their appeal for Canadians preoccupied with the problems of a rapidly industrializing society. George Denison sensed, in fact, that Canada was changing perhaps too rapidly for his liking. 'I do not care for Toronto as I

used to do,' he confided to Mair on New Year's eve, 1911: 'It
has changed and is changing every day. ... It is not the same
place it was thirty years ago. ... Parvenues are as plentiful as
blackberries and the vulgar ostentation of the common rich is
not a pleasant sight.'[28] A high board fence erected around Heydon Villa helped to preserve something of Toronto's earlier more
bucolic, atmosphere and Denison increasingly devoted his spare
time to his gardens. Nevertheless, he was forced to come to grips
with the new Toronto every day in his police court, where he
continued to mete out justice until a few months prior to his
82nd birthday. Even then he retired only under duress, still
campaigning for legal reforms to protect individuals from the
excessive costs of litigation which put justice beyond the reach
of the common man.

In this, as in other respects, he remained Toronto's 'grand old
man' testily championing causes dear to him. At 75, he contem-
plated volunteering for active duty overseas in the First World
War. An ardent supporter of conscription, Denison was an
equally outspoken critic of Borden's minister of militia, Sam
Hughes, and of the armistice which ended the war before Ger-
many had been smashed and the Kaiser hanged as a war criminal.
It was a characteristic response from a man whose own family
was decimated by the conflict. True to their traditions, more
than a dozen of 'the fighting Denisons' served in Europe. Among
those who did not return was George Taylor Denison (4th).

When George Denison (3rd) died, after a brief illness, on Sat-
urday, 6 June 1925, the nation's newspapers strove to outdo
one another in their respective eulogies. One, the Victoria *Daily
Colonist*, announced simply 'Denison is dead.' All who read it
understood the implication. Not merely a man, but an era had

passed into history. Even in his own lifetime the causes for which he crusaded had prompted a younger generation of Canadians with different preoccupations, for whom J.W. Dafoe is a convenient spokesman, to wonder if Colonel Denison was not responsible for some 'queer ideas about Canada.' Dafoe, the editor of the Manitoba *Free Press*, found it 'nauseating' that many Canadians had been led to believe that Canada 'was saved from toppling over into the arms of the United States by the wonderful loyalty and vigilance of individuals ... like Colonel Denison ... who sit up at night on guard, with clenched teeth, determined to keep Canada British. ...'[29] But if he appeared to Dafoe's generation as an atavistic Don Quixote championing long-forgotten causes, George Denison nevertheless shared and reflected the attitudes of the Confederation generation. They inherited and helped to shape a historical tradition embodying the tensions and strains of an incipient nation caught between the two competing poles of North American civilization.

These 'Victorian' Canadians admired and envied the United States of America for its material progress, but they feared its 'manifest destiny' and they disdained its revolutionary political, social, and moral doctrines which threatened to 'destroy civilization and bring about a return to barbarism' through an overdose of democracy. Similarly, they believed intensely in the 'greatness of progress ... and good accomplished' through the medium of the British Empire, and were even inclined to ascribe it to the 'extraordinary influence' of the example set by their monarch as Queen and mother.[30] But they were equally aware of the irreparable damage to their own interests which British statesmen, whether imperialist or anti-imperialist, had proved capable of inflicting from time to time. At any given moment, in short, the fortunes of the new Canadian political nationality reflected British North America's peculiar situation vis-à-vis her cultural parentage.

For most Victorian Canadians, maintaining the delicate balance of their precarious situation was a sufficient test of nationalism. George Denison, who had always been intrigued by the 'rise and fall of nations,' differed from his contemporaries because he delighted in seeing the balance challenged; out of tension, conflict, and struggle came the determination to survive. His own role was dictated by a genuine desire to influence, and direct, the development of a viable nationality. Discarding alternative vehicles of nationalism he turned to what he knew best, history and family tradition. Denison understood perhaps too well that the real test of Canadian nationality was its continuing ability to assert its independence in North America. The threat of failure was a constant condition of life after 1867, but it had been after 1776 as well and George Denison had learned the lessons of history and of family experience. He emerged as a Tory patriot defending the 'dream of the U.E. Loyalists' against the historical enemy, in fair weather or foul, *pour encourager les autres.* 'British connection is Colonel Denison's hobby,' stated one editor. 'He is the Queen's champion. ...'[31]

V

The Praetorian Guard

Bellevue, Rusholme, Dover Court, and Heydon Villa no longer stand in west Toronto to bear witness to the Denison family's former prominence as soldiers, citizens, and public men. But within earshot of the commercial and industrial din of Weston, Ontario, lies St. John's Cemetery, an unobtrusive link with the past. Established by George Denison of Bellevue, St. John's is the final resting place for all his descendants. Within its confines, however, special tribute is paid to those Denisons who have served King, Country, and Empire as soldiers. An imposing cenotaph stands as a continuing reminder that the Denisons have been a family of warriors whose record of service, spanning the history of Canada from fledgling colony to mature nation, established their right to an enduring place in the nation's history. Throughout the nineteenth century the Denisons were Upper Canada's, and the early Dominion's, praetorian guard.

A spirit of militant patriotism was at once the vehicle and the product of their place in the political and social hierarchy. Their firm conviction was that British North America's independence lay in successfully resisting the power of the United States of America, and in promoting the unity of the Empire as the essential counterpoise to continentalism. That conviction, rooted in the daily experience of the family and the country for a century and a half, created and perpetuated the praetorian impulse. In the colonial period of Canadian history, it carried the obligation to stand on guard for the young society whose survival and stability depended on its ability to defend itself from internal and external threats. As an example of practical loyalism for a political ideal and as an ever-present symbol of the counter-revolutionary origins of British North American nationality, the Denisons' military activities served as an essential buttress for colonial development. Later, the family's continuing dedication to the maintenance of a viable native defensive capacity helped to sustain a Canadian military tradition as a necessary precondition of nationhood. After 1867, though the threat of physical acts of aggression against the new nation gradually waned, the Denisons continued to hold themselves and their troop in readiness for the call to arms from the nation or the Empire. The two Riel rebellions, the Egyptian campaign of 1884-1885, the Boer War, and the First World War all saw Denisons actively engaged, and members of the family may still be found on the muster rolls of the British army.

But the praetorian spirit involved something more than a sword held ready in anticipation of a struggle for survival. It was also a state of mind, an absolute conviction that the objectives of the nation enjoyed historical sanction and required perpetual reinforcement. The household gods might be destroyed; they might as easily be forgotten, and the result could be a more insidious, but no less real threat to the 'dream of the United Empire Loyalists.' In the hands of George Taylor Denison (3rd), family tradition and the lessons of the past became a program of action designed to stimulate patriotism for Canada as the best possible defence against apathy and discouragement, and as the most vital weapon of national survival.

In retrospect, the measure of the Denison family's historical importance is neither the range nor the influence of their activities, collectively or as individuals. Other men have left a more definitive stamp on Canadian society either because they participated in it on a higher plane or because they altered the course of history through some dramatic personal involvement. What is unique about the Denisons is the remarkable unity of family tradition and experience throughout an era of Canadian history with an inherent unity of its own. The times conditioned the men, and the Denisons in turn mirrored the development of British North America from the beginnings of English settlement in Upper Canada to the emergence of an independent nation. Still, the conditions of the times and their own temperaments also foreordained a special historical role for the Denison family quite apart from their identification with the ordinary concerns of nineteenth century Canadians. As defenders of the spirit and the fact of Canadian nationality in their limited sphere as soldiers and publicists, the Denisons added the weight of their arms and voices to the perception of a distinct British North American identity and destiny that emerged at mid-century as the pole star of Canadian life.

The family's contribution to the pursuit of that destiny resides less in the magnitude than in the consistency of the Denisons' efforts. From 1792 until 1925 the Denisons of Toronto –

warriors, citizens and patriots – were self-styled champions of the Loyalist tradition in Canada; that tradition united, and gave meaning to, the experience of successive generations of Denisons, and they assumed it to be the spirit that breathed meaning into the historical experience of all Canadians, past, present, and future. For more than a century they laboured in the light of that assumption. Whether they were successful, indeed, whether they and those who sympathized with them were correct in their assumption, can be judged best in terms of our own assumptions about the meaning of nationality.

Notes

CHAPTER II

1 Ontario Archives (OA), Russell Papers, Denison to Russell, 11 June 1793.
2 *Ibid.*, Russell to William Jarvis, 10 March 1792.
3 *Ibid.*, Denison to Russell, 17 May 1793.
4 *Ibid.*, Denison to Russell, 23 June 1793, 26 May 1795; Russell to Denison, 10 June 1795; OA, A.T. Galt Papers, Statement of Accounts, Kingston Brewery (1794).
5 OA, Russell Papers, Denison to Russell, 14 November 1796.
6 *The Town of York, 1793-1815,* Edith G. Firth, ed., p.21; Henry Scadding, *Toronto of Old* (1966 ed.), pp.173-214, 248-249; G.T. Denison (2nd), *Chronicle of St. John's Cemetery-on-the-Humber;* G.M. Craig, *Upper Canada,* p.49; Public Archives of Canada (PAC), Denison Papers, 15, Certificate of land grant.
7 Claude H. Van Tyne, *The Loyalists of the American Revolution* (1959 ed.), p.174.
8 Varying accounts of this episode are to be found in North Callahan, *Royal Raiders,* pp.244-246 and Egerton Ryerson, *The Loyalists of America and Their Times,* II, 193-195. L.F.S. Upton's *The Loyal Whig* contains an account of the judicial proceedings from Smith's vantage point. The present account is drawn primarily from Public Record Office, America and West Indies Papers, 145, pp.31-46 (copy in PAC, Denison Papers, 15).
9 G.F.G. Stanley, *Canada's Soldiers,* rev. ed., p.149; J.M. Hitsman, *The Incredible War of 1812,* pp.36-37; G.T. Denison, *Soldiering in Canada,* pp.20-21.
10 *The Town of York, 1815-1834,* Edith G. Firth, ed., p.338; Ernest J. Chambers, *The Governor-General's Body Guard,* p.29.

11 Frederick C. Denison, *Historical Record of the Governor-General's Body Guard and Its Standing Orders,* pp.12-13; Chambers, pp.29-33; George T. Denison (2nd), 'The Burning of the "Caroline,"' *Canadian Monthly and National Review,* III (April 1873), 289-292.

12 Charles Lindsey, *The Life and Times of William Lyon Mackenzie,* II, 360. The manifesto was issued a fortnight before the rebellion.

13 See F.H. Armstrong, 'The Carfrae Family,' *Ontario History,* LIV (1962), 181.

14 OA, A.T. Galt Papers, Sophia Denison to George Taylor Denison, 15 March 1826.

15 Samuel Thompson, *Reminiscences of a Canadian Pioneer for the Last Fifty Years,* p.166; Scadding, p.258; J.G. Fleming, 'The Fighting Denisons,' *Maclean's Magazine,* XXVII (December 1913), 9; an excellent reproduction of Bellevue appears in Eric Arthur, *Toronto: No Mean City,* p.33.

16 OA, O'Brien Journal, 29, 24 June 1830; Thompson, p.166; Scadding, 'Editor's Introduction,' p.23; Henry Scadding and John Charles Dent, *Toronto: Past and Present,* p.28; F.H. Armstrong, 'William Lyon Mackenzie: First Mayor of Toronto,' *Canadian Historical Review,* XLVIII (December 1967), 309-331.

17 G.T. Denison, *Chronicle;* Thompson, p.166; Scadding, p.259; PAC, Denison Papers, 23, Diary, 29 July 1851.

18 C.C. Taylor, *Toronto 'Called Back,'* p.30.

19 Thompson, pp.170-171; *Dominion Annual Register, 1878* p.340; Toronto *Globe,* 11 March 1878.

20 *Dominion Annual Register, 1881,* p.365.

21 Metropolitan Toronto Central Library (MTCL), Denison Papers, G.L. Strachan to G.T. Denison, 3 April 1837; affidavit of G.T. Denison (2nd), 1839; legal and household accounts of G.T. Denison (2nd); estate books, G.T. Denison (1st); PAC, Denison Papers, 23, Diary, 1850-1855.

22 MTCL, Denison Papers, legal and household accounts, 1850-1860.

23 PAC, Denison Papers, 23, Diary, 11 September 1854.

24 *Ibid.,* 23 and 24, Diaries, 1850-1863.

25 *Ibid.,* 23, Diary, 1 July 1851.

26 See C.F. Hamilton, 'Defence, 1812-1912,' *Canada and Its Provinces,* VII, 391-405; and R.A. Preston, *Canada and 'Imperial Defense,'* pp.53-54.

27 Frederick Denison, p.14.

28 PAC, RG9, IC1, vol. 291, G.T. Denison (2nd) to Sir E.P. Taché, 4 April 1864.

29 *A Review of the Militia Policy of the Present Administration,* by Junius, Jr., pp.7-8.

30 PAC, Denison Papers, 1, G.T. Denison (3rd) to Lord Monck, 18 April 1866 [draft]; MacDougall to Denison, 26 April 1866.

31 Colonial Office, CO 42, vol. 678, pp.240-245, Sir John Young to Lord Grenville, No. 161, 20 December 1869 enc.: 'Petition of Col. Geo. Taylor Denison II to Queen Victoria.'

32 Toronto *Globe and Mail,* 10 March 1939; MTCL, Denison Papers, G.T. Denison (2nd) to Governor-General's military secretary, 24 July 1866.
33 PAC, Earl of Minto Papers, Hutton to Minto, 27 March 1901.
34 Toronto *Globe and Mail,* 9 November 1937.
35 Toronto *News,* 15 April 1896; *Commemorative Biographical Record of the County of York, Ontario,* p.192.
36 See Julian Symons, *England's Pride: The Story of the Gordon Relief Expedition,* pp.8-13; Lord Elton, *Gordon of Khartoum,* p.274; John Morley, *The Life of William Ewart Gladstone,* II, 384-386.
37 Sir E.H. Colvile, *History of the Sudan Campaign,* I, 29.
38 *Ibid.,* 43.
39 PAC, G19, vol. 34, Lambert to Melgund, 26 August 1884; vol. 50, Engagement Forms; PAC, G21, vol. 1, No. 162, Lansdowne to Derby, 12 September 1884 [draft]; PAC, Denison Papers, 3, F.C. Denison to G.T. Denison, 3 October 1884; Toronto *Globe,* 26 August, 15 September 1884; Colvile, II, Appendix 4, 188. See also the useful nominal roll appended to *The Nile Voyageurs, 1884-1885,* C.P. Stacey, ed., pp.256-258.
40 PAC, G19, vol. 38, Septimus Denison to Melgund, 26 August 1884; PAC, Denison Papers, 3, Egerton Denison to G.T. Denison, (?) September 1884; Toronto *Globe,* 17 September 1884.
41 MTCL, Denison Papers, Diary, 14 September–5 October 1884 (hereinafter cited as 'Nile Diary').
42 Colvile, I, 117.
43 Nile Diary, 2 November 1884; Toronto *Globe,* 15 September 1884; PAC, Denison Papers, 3, F.C. Denison to G.T. Denison, 25 December 1884.
44 MTCL, Denison Papers, F.C. Denison to John Denison, 10 November 1884; to Julia Denison, 21 November 1884; to Wolseley, 13 December 1884.
45 Sir William F. Butler, *Campaign of the Cataracts,* p.300; Colvile, II, 81-85; Major-General Henry Brackenbury, *The River Column,* pp.1-4; PAC, G19, vol. 34, Denison to Melgund, 10 January 1885.
46 Nile Diary, 1-9 February 1885; MTCL, Denison Papers, F.C. Denison to Julia Denison, 6 February 1885.
47 PAC, Denison Papers, 3, F.C. Denison to G.T. Denison, 1 February 1885.
48 *Ibid.,* 12 February 1885.
49 Brackenbury, p.246.

CHAPTER III

1 PAC, Denison Papers, 17, 'Phrenological Character of Mr. George T. Denison Given at Fowler and Wells' Phrenological Cabinet 1 November 1859.'

2 *Ibid.*, 27, Diary, 31 August 1879.
3 George T. Denison, 'A Visit to General Robert E. Lee,' *Canadian Monthly and National Review,* I (March 1872), 237.
4 George T. Denison, *Modern Cavalry: Its Organisation, Armament and Employment in War,* p.17.
5 PAC, Denison Papers, 26, Diary, 31 August 1864.
6 *Minutes of Proceedings of the Council of the Corporation of the City of Toronto ... 1865* (Toronto: Leader and Patriot Steam Press, 1866), pp.58-59. North Callahan, *Royal Raiders,* p.244 makes the point that Lippincott's gallows probably consisted of three fence rails and a flour barrel.
7 Accounts of the events that follow are to be found in Guy McLean, 'The *Georgian* Affair: An Incident of the American Civil War,' *Canadian Historical Review,* XLII (June 1961), 133-144; Robin Winks, *Canada and the United States: The Civil War Years,* pp.297 ff.; and John W. Headley, *Confederate Operations in Canada and New York,* pp.227-275. However, in order to reconstruct this incident and to arrive at a more comprehensive explanation of Denison's role, I have relied heavily on the evidence given in *Denison* v. *Collector of Customs* and *The United States* v. *Denison et al.,* complete reports and transcripts of which appear in PAC, MG27 IH3, reels M606, M668, M669, and in PAC, RG7, G6, vol. 14. These records include the reports of American consuls in Canada to the State Department, and the correspondence between the British minister in Washington and the governor-general of British North America.
8 PAC, Sir John A. Macdonald Papers, Denison to Macdonald, 9 May, 30 June, 13 August 1867; PAC, Denison Papers, 1, Macdonald to Denison, 10, 14 August 1867.
9 PAC, Denison Papers, 1, Denison to Macdonald, 9 May 1867.
10 University of Western Ontario (UWO), James Coyne Papers, Morgan to Coyne, 10 February 1890.
11 R.G. Haliburton, *The Men of the North and their Place in History,* p.1.
12 *Ibid.,* pp.2-10; Queen's University, Charles Mair Papers (Mair Papers), Denison to Mair, 10 March, 8 June 1869.
13 Joseph Schumpeter, *Social Classes: Imperialism,* pp.7-21.
14 Toronto *Globe,* 15 September 1870.
15 PAC, Denison Papers, 18, *Election Manifesto.*
16 Toronto *Globe,* 25 April 1872.
17 'The Late Session of the Parliament of Ontario,' *Canadian Monthly and National Review,* I (April 1872), 322. G.T. Denison, *The Struggle for Imperial Unity,* p.58. The *Canadian Monthly* was founded by a group of young men who sympathized with Canada First's ideals, and the magazine became an outlet for Canada First propaganda, particularly through the columns written by Goldwin Smith.
18 UWO, Coyne Papers, Foster to Coyne, 30 September 1873.

19 Mair Papers, Foster to Mair, 10 June 1875. For press reaction to the Canada First party see W.A. Foster's 'Canada First Scrapbook' (Canadian Library Association microfilm).

20 Mair Papers, Denison to Mair, 20 February 1876.

21 PAC, Denison Papers, 27, Diary, 31 August 1879.

22 *Ibid.*, 9, Denison to Helen Denison, 30 April, 8 May 1900; OA, Denison's Letter-book, 1872-1874.

23 Colonel Patrick L. MacDougall, *Modern Warfare as Influenced by Modern Artillery*, pp. 13-15; and see Captain L.E. Nolan, *Cavalry: Its History and Tactics*, 2nd ed.

24 *The Broad Arrow*, XXVII (28 September, 1868), 313-314; George T. Denison, 'Cavalry Charges at Sedan,' *Canadian Monthly and National Review*, I (January 1872), 49.

25 PAC, Denison Papers, 2, Mary Tangate to Denison, 24 February 1878.

26 *Ibid.*, Leontieff to Denison, 18 August 1877, my translation (original in French).

27 Mair Papers, Denison to Mair, 11 January 1879.

28 'A Law Reformer,' *Canada Law Journal*, XXXVI (October 1900), 517-520; 'A Dollar and Costs,' *Canada Monthly*, XIV (August 1913), 11; Harry Wodson, *The Whirlpool*, pp.24-32; 'A Lawyer on Lawyers' Fees,' *Canadian Journal of Commerce* (September 1890), 870; Mair Papers, Denison to Mair, 31 December 1911.

29 Mair Papers, Denison to Mair, 27 March, 30 March 1885; PAC, Denison Papers, 27, Diary, April-June 1885.

30 PAC, Denison Papers, 27, Diary, 1 December 1887; Mair Papers, Denison to Mair, 14 January, 25 April 1888.

CHAPTER IV

1 OA, William Kirby Collection, Denison to Kirby, 1 September 1888.

2 Mair Papers, Denison to Mair, 30 December 1888. For the Commercial Union agitation see R.C. Brown, 'The Commercial Unionists in Canada and the United States,' Canadian Historical Association, *Report* (1963), pp.106-114.

3 PAC, Denison Papers, 4, Mair to Denison, 20 November 1888.

4 Kirby Collection, Denison to Kirby, 1 September 1888.

5 Mair Papers, Denison to Mair, 30 December 1888.

6 Toronto *Globe*, 1 November 1888, 14 January 1889.

7 Macdonald Papers, 332, Denison to Macdonald, 'Private and Confidential Memorandum on the Militia' (1890); PAC, Denison Papers, 20, contains a copy of *Raise the Flag*.

8 Toronto *Empire*, 18 December 1891.

9 Goldwin Smith, *Loyalty, Aristocracy and Jingoism*, pp.10-36; Toronto *Globe*, 10 November 1891.

10 Toronto *Empire,* 18 December 1891.
11 Toronto *Globe,* 17 January 1895.
12 PAC, Denison Papers, 5, Imperial Federation League, *Report of Special Committee ... 1892; Imperial Federation,* VII (March, 1892), 71; PAC, Denison Papers, 5, Arthur Loring to Denison, 27 June, 13 July 1891; E.M. Saunders, ed., *The Life and Letters of the Rt. Hon. Sir Charles Tupper,* II, 170-171.
13 PAC, Denison Papers, 7, Denison to Lord Salisbury, 1 May 1897 [draft].
14 PAC, Sir John Willison Papers, 22, Denison to Willison, 17 September 1898.
15 Toronto *Globe,* 18 March, 7 April 1899.
16 Denison, *Struggle for Imperial Unity,* p.277.
17 Toronto *Globe,* 2 October 1899.
18 PAC, Denison Papers, 9, Laurier to Denison, 3 November 1899.
19 André Siegfried, *The Race Question in Canada,* ed. F.H. Underhill, p.203.
20 Kirby Collection, Denison to Kirby, 22 March 1902.
21 PAC, Denison Papers, C.F. Murray (Secretary of the British Empire League) to Denison, 11 September 1901.
22 PAC, Sir Sandford Fleming Papers, 13, Denison to Fleming, 26 July 1902.
23 *Ibid.,* Denison to Fleming, 10 November 1905.
24 PAC, Denison Papers, 11, Bourassa to Denison, 11 September 1903.
25 Carl Berger, *The Sense of Power,* p.108.
26 PAC, Denison Papers, 13, Denison to Chamberlain, 18 March 1911 [copy].
27 *Ibid.,* Denison to Chamberlain, 7 October 1911 [draft].
28 Mair Papers, Denison to Mair, 31 December 1911; PAC, Denison Papers, 13, Denison to Chamberlain, 29 January 1910 [draft].
29 Manitoba *Free Press,* 27 July 1909, 19 January 1909.
30 Kirby Collection, Denison to Kirby, 25 March 1897; Toronto *Star,* 23 January 1901.
31 Ottawa *Citizen,* 23 September 1895.

Selected bibliography

This study was written primarily from the extensive manuscript sources cited below. Therefore, in keeping with the spirit of the editors' plea for brevity of citation, I have included in the bibliography only those secondary materials cited in the text, and those which seem fundamental to a selected bibliography of the Denison family and their times. Documentation throughout the text is equally brief, for similar reasons.

MANUSCRIPT SOURCES

Cornell University
  Goldwin Smith Papers
Public Archives of Canada
  Adjutant General's Office, Correspondence, 1846-1869 (RG9, IC1)
  Denison Papers
  Diary, Colonel F.C. Denison, 1884-1885 (microfilm)
  Despatches from British Minister at Washington (G6)
  Despatches to Colonial Office (G12)
  Despatches, U.S. Consuls in Canada (MG27, IH3)
  Sir Sandford Fleming Papers
  Governor-General's Numbered Files (G21)
  Laurier Papers

Macdonald Papers
Earl of Minto Papers (microfilm)
Henry J. Morgan Papers
Records of the Governor-General's Military Secretary (G19)
Willison Papers
Public Archives of Ontario
  Percy Band Collection
  G.T. Denison Letterbook
  A.T. Galt Papers
  William Kirby Collection
  Peter Russell Papers
Queen's University
  Charles Mair Papers
Metropolitan Toronto Central Library
  Denison Papers
University of Western Ontario
  James Coyne Papers

WORKS BY THE DENISON FAMILY

Denison, Frederick C. *Historical Record of the Governor General's Body Guard and Its Standing Orders.* Toronto: Hunter, Rose & Co., 1876
Denison, G.T. (2nd) 'The Burning of the "Caroline,"' *Canadian Monthly and National Review,* III (April 1873), 289-292
– *Chronicle of St. John's Cemetery-on-the-Humber.* Toronto, 1861
Denison, G.T. (3rd). 'Canada and the Imperial Conference,' *The Nineteenth Century and After,* LI (June 1902), 901-907
– *Canada: Is She Prepared for War?* Toronto, 1861
– 'Cavalry Charges at Sedan,' *Canadian Monthly and National Review,* I (January 1872), 47-53
– *History of the Fenian Raid on Fort Erie; with an Account of the Battle of Ridgeway.* Toronto, 1866
– *A History of Cavalry from the Earliest Times with Lessons for the Future.* London: Macmillan Co., 1877
– *Modern Cavalry: Its Organisation, Armament and Employment in War.* London: Thomas Bosworth, 1868

Selected bibliography

- *The National Defences; or, Observations on the Best Defensive Force for Canada.* Toronto, 1861
- *Recollections of a Police Magistrate.* Toronto: Musson, 1921
- *Reminiscences of the Red River Rebellion.* Toronto, 1873
- *A Review of the Militia Policy of the Present Administration.* By Junius, Jr., Hamilton, 1863
- *Soldiering in Canada.* Toronto: G.N. Morang, 1900
- *The Struggle for Imperial Unity.* Toronto: Macmillan Co., 1909
- 'A Visit to General Robert E. Lee,' *Canadian Monthly and National Review,* I (March 1872), 231-237
Denison, R.L. *The Canadian Pioneer Denison Family of County York, England and County York, Ontario,* 4 vols. Toronto: The Author, 1951-1953

PRINTED PRIMARY SOURCES

Chadwick, E.M. *Ontarian Families.* Toronto: Rolph, Smith & Co., 1894
Foster, W.A. 'Canada First Scrapbook.' Canadian Library Association microfilm
The Petition of George Taylor Denison, Jr., to the Honourable House of Assembly, Praying Redress in the Matter of the Steamer 'Georgian'. ... Toronto: Leader and Patriot Steam Press, 1865
Report of Cases Adjudged in Chancery Chambers, vol. 2. C.W. Cooper, Reporter. Toronto: Henry Rowsell, 1870
Stacey, C.P. *The Nile Voyageurs, 1884-1885.* Toronto: Publications of the Champlain Society, 1959
The Town of York, 1793-1815: A Collection of Documents of Early Toronto. Edith G. Firth, ed. Toronto: University of Toronto Press, 1962
The Town of York, 1815-1834. Edith G. Firth, ed. Toronto: University of Toronto Press, 1966
United States War Department. *War of the Rebellion: Official Records of the Union and Confederate Armies,* series IV, vol. 3. Washington: U.S. Gov't Printing Office, 1900

Selected bibliography

NEWSPAPERS AND JOURNALS

British Empire Review
Empire, Toronto
Globe, Toronto
Globe and Mail, Toronto
Imperial Federation
Leader, Toronto
Mail, Toronto
Nation, Toronto
The News, Toronto
Toronto Daily Star
Toronto Telegram
Winnipeg Free Press

SECONDARY SOURCES

A. BOOKS

Arthur, Eric. *Toronto: No Mean City*. Toronto: University of Toronto Press, 1964

Beresford, Admiral Lord Charles. *The Memoirs of Admiral Lord Charles Beresford*. London: Methuen, 1914

Berger, Carl. *The Sense of Power*. Toronto: University of Toronto Press, 1970

Brackenbury, Major-General Henry. *The River Column*. London: William Blackwood and Sons, 1885

Brown, R.C. *Canada's National Policy, 1883-1900*. Princeton: Princeton University Press, 1964

The British Empire League in Canada. Toronto: Carswell Co., 1897

Butler, Sir W.F. *The Campaign of the Cataracts*. London: Sampson and Low, 1887

– *Sir William Butler: An Autobiography*. Toronto: Bell and Cockburn, n.d.

Callahan, North. *Royal Raiders*. New York: Bobbs-Merrill, 1963

Canada at the Universal Exposition of 1855. Toronto: John Lovell, 1856

Chambers, Ernest J. *The Governor-General's Body Guard*. Toronto: E.L. Ruddy, 1902

Colvile, Sir E.H. *History of the Sudan Campaign,* 2 vols. London: H.M. Stationery Office, 1899

Commemorative Biographical Record of the County of York, Ontario. Toronto: J.M. Beers, 1907

Craig, G.M., ed. *Early Travellers in the Canadas, 1791-1867.* Toronto: Macmillan Co., 1955

– *Upper Canada: The Formative Years, 1784-1841.* Toronto: McClelland and Stewart, 1963

D'Arcy McGee, 1825-1925. Hon. Chas. Murphy, ed. Toronto: Macmillan Co., 1937

Davis, Samuel B. *Escape of a Confederate Officer from Prison.* Norfolk: Landmark Pub. Co., 1892

Dominion Annual Register, 1878-1886. Montreal and Toronto: various publishers, 1878-1887

Elton, Godfrey, Lord. *Gordon of Khartoum: The Life of General Charles George Gordon.* New York: Knopf, 1955

Foster, W.A. *Canada First; or, Our New Nationality.* Toronto: Adam, Stevenson & Co., 1871

Haliburton, R.G. *The Men of the North and their Place in History.* Montreal: John Lovell, 1869

Headley, John W. *Confederate Operations in Canada and New York.* New York: Neale Pub. Co., 1906

Hitsman, J.M. *The Incredible War of 1812: A Military History.* Toronto: University of Toronto Press, 1965

Horan, James T. *Confederate Agent: A Discovery in History.* New York: Crown Pub. Co., 1954

Imperial Federation: Report of Speech Delivered by Col. Geo. T. Denison ... March 29, 1890. Toronto: Imperial Federation League, 1890

Jomini. *Summary of the Art of War.* J.D. Hittle, ed. Harrisburg: Military Service Pub. Co., 1958

Keith, A.B. *Selected Speeches and Documents on British Colonial Policy, 1763-1917.* London: Oxford University Press, 1961

Kohn, Hans. *The Idea of Nationalism.* New York: Macmillan Co., 1966

Lindsey, Charles. *The Life and Times of William Lyon Mackenzie,* 2 vols. Toronto: P.R. Randall, 1862

Luvaas, Jay. *The Education of an Army.* Chicago: University of Chicago Press, 1964

– *The Military Legacy of the Civil War: The European Inheritance.* Chicago: University of Chicago Press, 1959

MacDougall, Col. P.L. *Modern Warfare as Influenced by Modern Artillery.* London: John Murray, 1864

Maurice, Major-General Sir F., and Sir George Arthur. *The Life of Lord Wolseley.* London: Heinemann, 1924

Morley, John. *The Life of William Ewart Gladstone,* 2 vols. London: Macmillan Co., 1922

Nelson, W.H. *The American Tory.* Oxford: Clarendon Press, 1961

Nolan, Capt. L.E. *Cavalry: Its History and Tactics.* Second edition. London: Thos. Bosworth, 1854

Penlington, Norman. *Canada and Imperialism, 1896-1899.* Toronto, 1965

Preston, R.A. *Canada and 'Imperial Defense.'* Durham, N.C.: Duke University Press, 1967

Ropp, Theodore. *War in the Modern World.* Rev. ed. New York: Collier Books, 1962

Royal Colonial Institute, *Proceedings,* vol. 33. London: Royal Colonial Institute, 1902

Ryerson, Egerton. *The Loyalists of America and Their Times: From 1620-1816,* 2 vols. Toronto: William Briggs, 1880

Scadding, Henry. *Toronto of Old.* F.H. Armstrong, ed. Toronto: Oxford University Press, 1966

– and John Charles Dent. *Toronto: Past and Present.* Toronto: Hunter, Rose and Co., 1884

Schumpeter, Joseph. *Social Classes: Imperialism.* New York: Meridian Books, 1964

Shrive, F.N. *Charles Mair: Literary Nationalist.* Toronto: University of Toronto Press, 1965

Siegfried, André. *The Race Question in Canada.* F.H. Underhill, ed. Toronto: McClelland and Stewart, 1966

Smith, Goldwin. *The Political Destiny of Canada.* Toronto: Willing and Williamson, 1878

– *Loyalty, Aristocracy and Jingoism.* Toronto: Hunter, Rose & Co., 1896

Stacey, C.P. *Canada and the British Army: A Study in the Practice of Responsible Government.* Rev. ed. Toronto: University of Toronto Press, 1963

Stanley, George F.G. *Canada's Soldiers: The Military History of an Unmilitary People.* Rev. ed. Toronto: Macmillan Co., 1960

Symons, Julian. *England's Pride: The Story of the Gordon Relief Expedition*. London: Hamish Hamilton, 1965

Thompson, Samuel. *Reminiscences of a Canadian Pioneer for the Last Fifty Years*. Toronto: Hunter, Rose & Co., 1884

Taylor, C.C. *Toronto 'Called Back,' from 1892 to 1847*. Toronto: William Briggs, 1897

Tyler, J.E. *The Struggle for Imperial Unity*. London: Longmans, Green, 1938

Underhill, F.H. *The Image of Confederation*. Toronto: Canadian Broadcasting Corp., 1964

Van Tyne, Claude H. *The Loyalists in the American Revolution*. Reprint. Gloucester, Mass.: Peter Smith, 1959

Wallace, Elisabeth. *Goldwin Smith: Victorian Liberal*. Toronto: University of Toronto Press, 1957

Warner, Donald F. *The Idea of Continental Union*. Louisville: University of Kentucky Press, 1960

Who's Who and Why, 1917-18. Toronto: International Press, 1919

Winks, Robin. *Canada and the United States: The Civil War Years*. Baltimore: Johns Hopkins Press, 1960

Wodson, Harry. *The Whirlpool*. Toronto, 1917

Wolseley, Field Marshal Viscount. *The American Civil War: An English View*. James A. Rawley, ed. Charlottesville: University Press of Virginia, 1964

– *The Story of a Soldier's Life*, 2 vols. New York: Scribner's, 1903

Woodham-Smith, Cecil. *The Reason Why*. London: McGraw-Hill, 1953

B. ARTICLES

Armstrong, F.H. 'The Carfrae Family: A Study in Early Toronto Toryism,' *Ontario History*, LIV (1962), 161-181

Armstrong, F.H. 'William Lyon Mackenzie, First Mayor of Toronto: A Study of a Critic in Power,' *Canadian Historical Review*, XLVIII (December 1967), 309-331

Black, Robson. 'A Dollar and Costs,' *Canada Monthly*, XIV (August 1913), 9-11

Brown, R.C. 'The Commercial Unionists in Canada and the United States,' *Canadian Historical Association, Annual Report*. Toronto: University of Toronto Press, 1963, pp.116-124

Selected bibliography

Fleming, J.G. 'The Fighting Denisons,' *Maclean's Magazine,* XXVII
(December 1913), 5-11
Hamilton, C.F. 'Defence, 1812-1912,' *Canada and Its Provinces,* vol. VII.
Toronto: Glasgow, Brook and Co., 1914, pp.391-405
McLean, G.L. 'The *Georgian* Affair: An Incident of the American Civil
War,' *Canadian Historical Review,* XLII (June 1961), 133-144
'A Lawyer on Lawyers' Fees,' *Canadian Journal of Commerce* (September
1890), 810
'A Law Reformer,' *Canada Law Journal,* XXXVI (October 1900), 517-520
Stacey, C.P. 'Canada and the Nile Expedition of 1884-85,' *Canadian
Historical Review,* XXXIII (December 1952), 319-340

Index

111

Index